Twosey–Foursey Quilts

Great Designs from 2-Inch and 4-Inch Units

Cathy Wierzbicki

Martingale®
& COMPANY

Twosey-Foursey Quilts:
Great Designs from 2-Inch and 4-Inch Units
© 2006 by Cathy Wierzbicki

 That Patchwork Place

That Patchwork Place® is an imprint of
Martingale & Company®.

Martingale & Company
20205 144th Avenue NE
Woodinville, WA 98072-8478 USA
www.martingale-pub.com

Credits

President • Nancy J. Martin
CEO • Daniel J. Martin
COO • Tom Wierzbicki
Publisher • Jane Hamada
Editorial Director • Mary V. Green
Managing Editor • Tina Cook
Technical Editor • Darra Williamson
Copy Editor • Liz McGehee
Design Director • Stan Green
Illustrator • Laurel Strand
Cover Designer • Regina Girard
Text Designer • Shelly Garrison
Photographer • Brent Kane

Printed in China

11 10 09 08 07   8 7 6 5 4 3 2

Library of Congress Cataloging-in-Publication Data

Library of Congress Control Number: 2006014372
ISBN-13: 978-1-56477-688-4
ISBN-10: 1-56477-688-3

Mission Statement
Dedicated to providing quality products
and service to inspire creativity.

Acknowledgments

Each of the following has been a blessing to me in
the making of this book, and I extend my heartfelt
thanks and appreciation to:

My mom, Shirley Sullivan, of West Branch,
Michigan, for helping with sewing and for her
ever-present enthusiasm and support.

Tamara Watts, Rita Bigelow, and Janeen
Pearson of Ankeny, Iowa, for piecing "Whisker
Burns," and Shelley Mitchell of Des Moines, Iowa,
for machine quilting it. What good friends they are!

Bonnie Gibbs of Zimmerman, Minnesota, for
her beautiful machine quilting on all but four of
these quilts.

All of the quilters at the 2005 fall retreat at Lake
Beauty in north-central Minnesota who willingly
made the blocks for "Retreat to the Lake," and to
Sue Herzberg of Quilt Cove, Eagan, Minnesota, for
inviting me to spend the weekend with her talented
and generous group.

The entire staff at Martingale & Company for
their dedication to excellence.

Contents

The Twosey-Foursey Way • 4

Alternative Cutting Options • 8

Helpful Quiltmaking Information • 11

The Quilts

Barbed Wire Fence • 14

Wild Goose Chase • 18

Blueberry Buckle • 22

Whistle While You Work • 26

Split the Difference • 30

Split the Difference Table Topper • 34

Plain and Fancy • 36

Whisker Burns • 40

Beginner's Delight • 44

Spinning Stars • 47

Splash Dance • 52

Amish Sparklers • 57

Cat Tracks • 60

Retreat to the Lake • 65

Roundabout • 68

Prairie Stars • 73

Bridging the Gap • 77

Leaf Chain Table Topper and Runners • 82

Feathered Foursome • 87

About the Author • 96

The Twosey-Foursey Way

I've done it before, and you probably have too: miscut a strip of fabric. A quick distraction, too many numbers to remember, an errant ruler alignment, aging eyesight—before you know it, you've just cut a lovely strip 4½" wide when what you really wanted was 4⅞". Ordinarily, that would necessitate cutting another strip, but not with Twosey-Foursey.

Welcome to the world of Twosey-Foursey. Read on and, in just two to four minutes, I'll answer all your Twosey-Foursey questions.

What Is Twosey-Foursey All About?

- A Twosey-Foursey is a patchwork piece that finishes at either 2" or 4".

- In a word, Twosey-Foursey means simplicity. By changing the way basic patchwork pieces are cut, quilters can concentrate less on cutting and more on sewing.

- Twosey-Foursey makes it possible to get a variety of shapes from strips of just two sizes: 2½" and 4½".

- Twosey-Foursey eliminates the need to work with ⅛" and ¼" measurements.

- With Twosey-Foursey, even half-square and quarter-square triangles can be cut from strips.

How Is Twosey-Foursey Easier?

Let's consider patchwork pieces that finish at 2". Traditionally, squares and rectangles are cut by adding ½" to the finished measurement of the pieces. For a square that finishes 2", you would cut a 2½" square. Likewise, for a rectangle that finishes 2" x 4", you would cut a 2½" x 4½" rectangle. Traditionally, half-square triangles are cut by adding ⅞" to the finished measurement of the piece. For a half-square triangle unit that finishes at 2", you would add ⅞" to the finished size, cut a square 2⅞", then subcut the square once diagonally. For a quarter-square triangle that finishes at 2" high and 4" wide,

you would add 1¼" to the finished size of the long edge, cut a square 5¼", then subcut the square twice diagonally. (I could give you the mathematical formula for this, but my guess is that your eyes are beginning to gloss over. It's understandable—you're suffering from number overload—2½", 2⅞", 5¼"—enough already!)

Twosey-Foursey makes it easy—just remember 2½". That's it. All of the pieces listed above can be cut from the same 2½" strip! It doesn't get any easier than that. And, if you're working with shapes that finish at 4", just remember 4½". How's that for simplicity?

How Do I Cut with the Twosey-Foursey Approach?

There are three ways to cut the pieces for the quilts in this book:

- With the aid of the All-in-One Ruler™—my preferred way

- With the aid of templates made from the patterns given in this book

- By resorting to traditional patchwork formulas for cutting (e.g., finished size of the short edges + ⅞" for half-square triangles; finished size of the long diagonal edge + 1¼" for quarter-square triangles)

The All-in-One Ruler

Whenever you set out to do a job, it always helps to have the right tools, and the All-in-One Ruler is the right tool for making the quilts in this book. The All-in-One Ruler is a comprehensive, all-purpose ruler designed to aid in cutting the most common shapes (e.g., squares, rectangles, half-square triangles, and quarter-square triangles) used by quiltmakers day in and day out. The ruler is *not* just for this book; in fact, its versatility makes it the perfect ruler for all basic quiltmaking. Here is how it works.

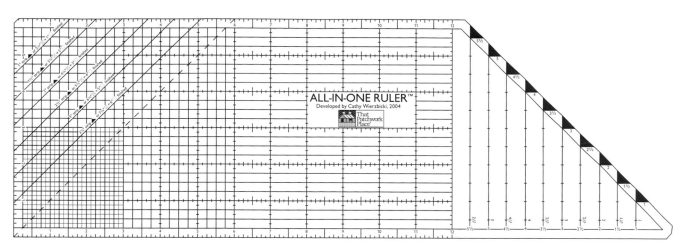

The All-in-One Ruler

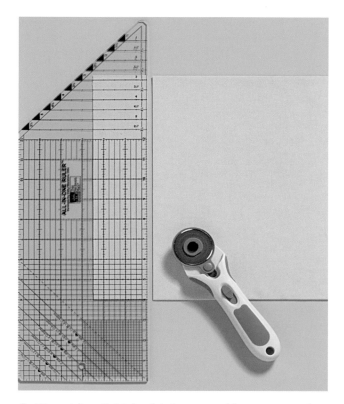

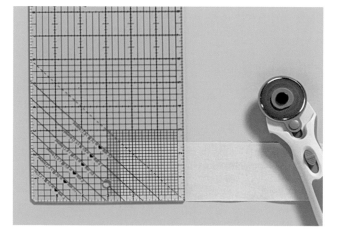

Cutting squares: Cut a strip to the width of the square you wish to cut, then crosscut the strip into squares, aligning the strip with the desired measurement on the ruler.

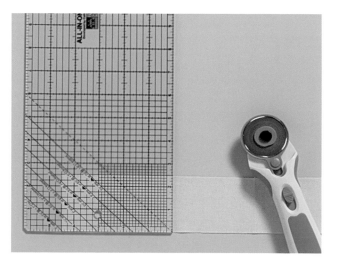

Cutting strips: Fold the fabric as usual for rotary cutting and place the folded fabric on a cutting mat. Position the ruler on the fabric, aligning the marking that matches the desired measurement with the cut edge of the fabric. Using a rotary cutter, run the blade along the long edge of the ruler.

Cutting rectangles: Cut a strip to the height of the rectangle you wish to cut, then crosscut the strip into rectangles, aligning the strip with the desired measurement on the ruler.

5

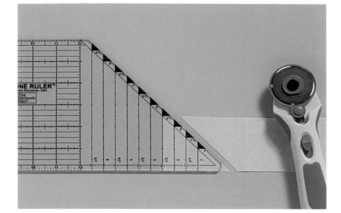

Cutting half-square triangles from strips: The All-in-One Ruler allows you to cut half-square triangles from strips, but the math is greatly simplified. You only need to add ½" to the finished measurement of the square instead of the traditional ⅞". For example, to cut half-square triangles that finish at 2", cut a strip that measures 2½" wide. Using the ruler's angled edge, position the ruler on top of the strip as shown and cut along the diagonal edge.

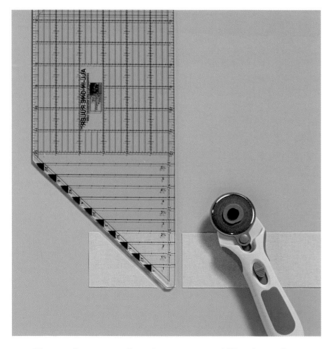

To cut the next triangle, rotate and flip the ruler to the right, reposition as shown, and cut along the right edge of the ruler. For this cut, the back side of the ruler is facing up. The ruler is marked with reverse printing, making the numbers easy to read from both sides. To make the next cut, return the ruler to the original position and repeat; continue in this manner across the strip.

The process is the same when you are working with 4½"-wide strips to cut half-square triangles. Simply substitute the 4½" markings on the ruler for the 2½" markings.

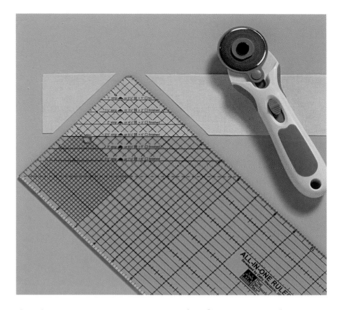

Cutting quarter-square triangles from strips: The printed diagonal lines show what size strip to use to arrive at the desired finished size. They also show the equivalent measurement you would need when cutting quarter-square triangles in the traditional manner. For example, a quarter-square triangle cut from a 2½" strip will finish at 4" wide. This is equivalent to cutting a 5¼" square, then cutting the square diagonally twice to yield four quarter-square triangles. Look at the fourth diagonal line from the corner of the ruler to see this illustrated on the ruler.

Once you cut a 2½" wide strip, align the notched corner of the ruler with the top edge of the fabric strip. The 2½" diagonal line of the ruler will naturally align with the bottom edge of the strip. Cut along both edges of the ruler

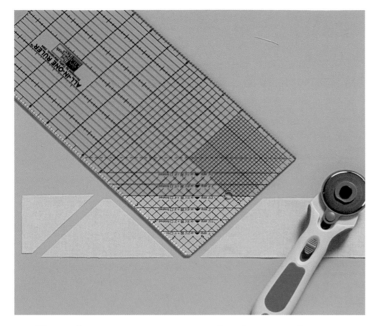

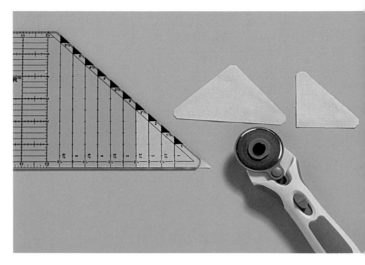

To cut the next quarter-square triangle, rotate the ruler so that the notched corner of the ruler aligns with the bottom edge of the fabric strip and the 2½" printed line aligns with the top edge of the strip. Cut along the right edge of the ruler. Continue in this manner across the strip.

Trimming points: Use the blunt point at the 45°-angled edges of the ruler to pretrim patchwork pieces before sewing. Trimming points allows you to align pieces easily, resulting in more accurate piecing. This is especially useful when piecing flying-geese units or dogtooth units.

To trim points, position the blunt point of the ruler on a triangle, aligning the angled and bottom edges of the ruler with those of the triangle. Cut the fabric that extends beyond the blunt point.

If you have trouble getting sharp points on your stars or flying-geese units, use the point trimmer. I have seen quiltmakers across the country go from making imprecise, decapitated flying geese to sewing razor-sharp points with great accuracy—simply because the points were trimmed prior to sewing.

Yes, you absolutely can be successful making these quilts without the All-in-One Ruler. Many of the quilts require nothing more than strips, squares, and rectangles—there's nothing unique about these shapes. For those quilts that include half-square triangles or quarter-square triangles, however, use either the templates included in the book or use the traditional rotary-cutting formulas.

Using Templates

The patterns on pages 9 and 10 are for making half-square and quarter-square triangles. (The notched corner on the quarter-square triangle and the blunt points on both triangles match these features on the All-in-One Ruler.) Trace the patterns onto template plastic, tagboard, or card stock. Cracker or cereal boxes are also great for this purpose. Position the templates onto the strips as shown below and at right and cut around the templates with your rotary cutter.

To cut half-square triangles, position the appropriately sized (2" or 4") triangle template on the appropriately sized strip, aligning the bottom edge of the template with the bottom edge of the fabric strip, and the left edge of the template with the cut edge of the strip. Carefully cut along the diagonal edge of the template.

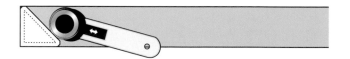

Reinforce the Template

If you wish, instead of cutting with the template alone, you can position your rotary ruler over the template and cut along the edge of the ruler.

To make the second cut, reposition the template so that the diagonal edge of the template is aligned with the cut edge of the fabric, the top of the template is aligned with the top of the strip, and one blunt point is pointing at you. Make a vertical cut along the edge of the template.

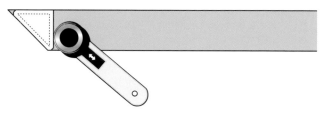

To continue cutting, place the template in the original position and proceed in a like manner across the strip.

To cut quarter-square triangles, position template on the strip, aligning the bottom of the template with the bottom of the strip and aligning the notched corner of the template with the top of the strip. Cut along both edges of the template.

To make another cut, reposition the template so that the notched corner is pointing toward you and is aligned with the bottom of the strip, the bottom of the template is aligned with the top of the strip, and the edge of the template is aligned with the diagonal cut edge of the fabric.

To continue cutting, place the template in the original position and proceed in a like manner across the strip.

Cutting the Traditional Way

Twosey-Foursey squares and rectangles can be cut from either 2½" strips or 4½" strips, depending on the pattern. However, if you prefer to cut triangles in the traditional manner, the following chart gives equivalent measurements. Keep in mind that you may need to make slight adjustments in the required yardages.

Finished Size	If Twosey-Foursey says to cut:	The traditional equivalent is:
2" square	2½" strip	2½" strip
4" square	4½" strip	4½" strip
2" half-square triangle	2½" strip	Cut a square 2⅞" x 2⅞", then cut the square diagonally once to yield two half-square triangles.
4" half-square triangle	4½" strip	Cut a square 4⅞" x 4⅞", then cut the square diagonally once to yield two half-square triangles.
Quarter-square triangle	2½" strip	Cut a square 5¼" x 5¼"; then cut the square diagonally twice to yield four quarter-square triangles.

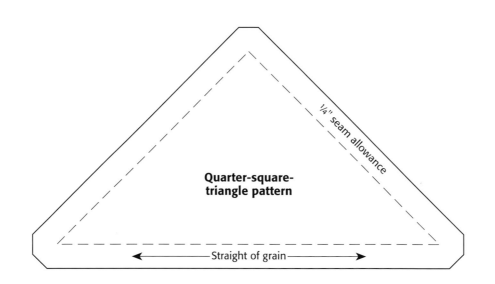

Quarter-square-triangle pattern

¼" seam allowance

←———— Straight of grain ————→

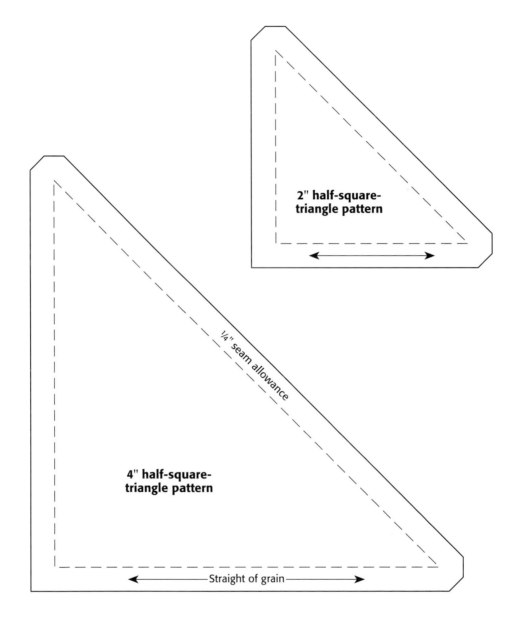

2" half-square-triangle pattern

¼" seam allowance

4" half-square-triangle pattern

Straight of grain

The following pages offer useful tips for streamlining the cutting and piecing of frequently used units, sewing an accurate ¼" seam allowance, and finishing the edges of your quilt with my preferred binding technique.

Making Flippy Corners

A "flippy corner" is a casual way to sew half-square triangles onto squares or rectangles without actually handling a triangle shape—cheater triangles, so to speak. This technique can be applied to a number of commonly used units and blocks. A good example is the flying-geese unit.

Three quilts in this book use traditionally made flying-geese units: "Prairie Stars" (page 73), "Feathered Foursome" (page 87), and "Plain and Fancy" (page 36). In each case, the pattern calls for one quarter-square triangle and two half-square triangles.

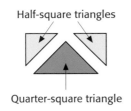

Half-square triangles

Quarter-square triangle

If you prefer, however, you can make flying-geese units using the flippy-corner technique as I did for "Splash Dance" (page 52). To do so, substitute a 2½" x 4½" rectangle for the quarter-square triangle, and two 2½" squares for the two half-square triangles. Make the unit as shown in the following steps.

1. Draw a diagonal line on the back of each 2½" square.

2½"

2. With right sides together, align one marked square with one edge of the 2½" x 4½" rectangle as shown. Stitch one thread width to the outside of the diagonal line.

3. Cut ¼" beyond the stitching line as shown. Press toward the triangle.

4. Repeat steps 2 and 3 on the other edge of the rectangle to complete the unit.

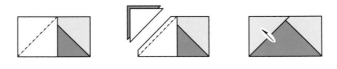

Testing Your Seam Allowance

Nothing affects quiltmaking success, or lack of it, quite like a ¼"-wide seam allowance. Each time you begin to sew, take a moment to check that you are stitching an accurate seam allowance.

1. Cut three scrap strips that measure 1½" x 3".

2. Using a ¼" seam allowance, sew the strips together along the long edges; press.

3. Measure the finished width of the center strip. If it is precisely 1", you passed the test. If the finished width is any measurement other than 1", adjust your seam allowance accordingly and retest.

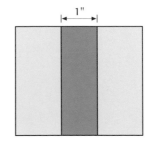

1"

Making Painless Mitered Binding

The binding technique presented here yields great-looking corners and eliminates the need to close up the edge of the binding with a pesky mitered seam. It works well with binding of any width. You do not need to make any adjustments when sewing; just cut the binding strips wider.

1. Place a chalk or pencil mark ¼" from each corner of the quilt top. Measure the quilt top between the marks and note these measurements; they will help you determine the length of the binding strips you need to make.

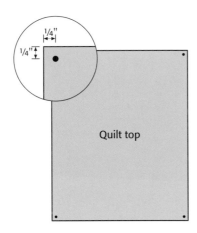

2. Cut strips of binding fabric as directed in the project instructions. For each edge of the quilt, you will need one strip that is approximately 6" longer than the edge to be bound. Using diagonal seams, join strips, if necessary, to make a long-enough strip.

3. Press the strips in half lengthwise, wrong sides together. With raw edges even, sew the appropriate folded strip to one edge of the quilt top, leaving approximately 3" of binding extending beyond each end. Begin sewing at the first chalk mark; stop sewing at the second chalk mark.

Backstitch to secure the ends of the strip. Repeat to sew a strip to each side of the quilt.

4. Place the quilt top on a flat surface with the raw edge of one binding strip facing you. Bring the folded edge toward you, stopping at the line of stitching; crease. Open up the binding and lay it flat again.

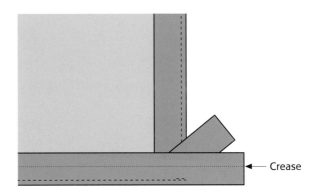
Crease

Alternative to the All-in-One Ruler

If you do not have an All-in-One Ruler, you can make a "miter marking guide" by drawing a diagonal line from corner to corner on a 3"-square self-stick note. Make seven or eight pencil marks at ⅛" intervals along two adjacent edges as shown. Using this marking guide as a substitute for the ruler, position the guide as explained above and proceed as follows.

5. Place an All-in-One Ruler on the binding strip, aligning the diagonal dashed line of the ruler on top of the crease mark on the binding. Position the ruler so that one of the ⅛" markings meets the folded edge of the binding, while another ⅛" marking meets the backstitch. There should be an equal number of marks from the tip of the ruler to the folded edge of the binding, and from the tip of the ruler to the backstitch.

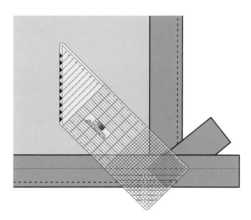

6. Using a pencil or chalk marker, trace around the tip of the ruler (or marking guide), drawing a line from the folded edge of the binding to the back-stitch. (Make sure the drawn line points *away* from the quilt.) Remove the ruler or guide. With the right side of the quilt facing up, fold the quilt diagonally from the corner so that the marked binding strip and the adjacent binding strip are aligned along the folded edges. Pin the binding strips together.

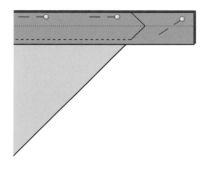

7. Sew along the marked line, starting at the folded edge and sewing to within one stitch of the tip. Stop, pivot, and take one stitch across the tip. Pivot again and continue stitching down the marked line to the backstitch. Trim ¼" away from the stitching line and turn the corner to the right side.

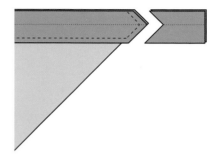

8. Repeat steps 4–7 for the remaining corners.

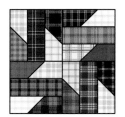

Finished quilt size: 60½" x 72½"
Finished unit size: 6" x 6"

Materials

Yardage is based on 42"-wide fabric. To make sure the secondary pattern pops in this design, maintain a sharp contrast between the light and dark fabrics.

- 4 yards *total* of assorted dark fabrics for block and border units
- 2 yards *total* of assorted light fabrics for block and border units
- ⅝ yard of fabric for binding
- 4½ yards of fabric for backing (vertical seam); 3⅔ yards (horizontal seam)
- 66" x 78" piece of batting
- 1 ball of pearl cotton, size 5 or 8

Cutting

All measurements include ¼"-wide seam allowances. Cut all strips across the width of the fabric.

Fabric	First Cut	Second Cut
Assorted darks	A *total* of 13 strips, 4½" wide	200 rectangles, 2½" x 4½" (A)
	A *total* of 27 strips, 2½" wide	160 rectangles, 2½" x 6½" (B)
Assorted lights	A *total* of 13 strips, 4½"wide	200 rectangles, 2½" x 4½" (C)
Binding	7 strips, 2½" wide	

Making the Block and Border Units

Refer to page 11 for tips on sewing an accurate ¼" seam allowance.

1. Referring to "Making Flippy Corners" on page 11 and with right sides together, position a C rectangle on top of an A rectangle at a right angle as shown. Sew, trim, and press. Make 200.

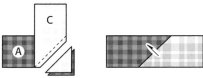

Make 200.

2. Sew a pieced unit from step 1 to each long side of one B rectangle, rotating one of the units as shown. Make 80.

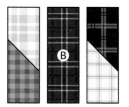

Make 80.

3. Arrange four units from step 2 as shown. Sew the units together to complete a large block; press. Make 20.

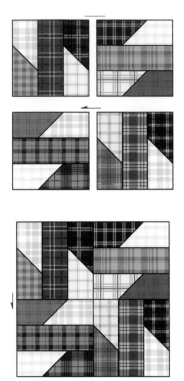

Make 20.

4. Sew a remaining pieced unit from step 1 and two remaining B rectangles together to make border units as shown. Make 40.

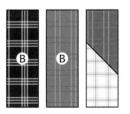 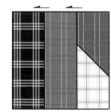

Make 40.

Assembling the Quilt

1. Arrange the large blocks in five horizontal rows of four blocks each as shown in the assembly diagram. Sew the blocks together into rows; press. Sew the rows together; press.

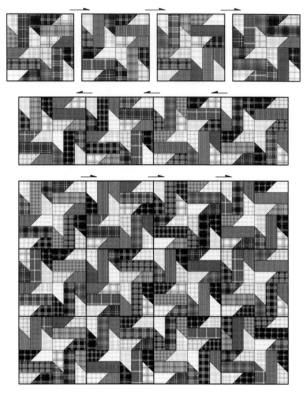

Assembly diagram

2. Beginning with a horizontally oriented block, arrange and sew 10 border units together, rotating them as shown; press. Make two for the side borders.

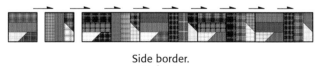

Side border.
Make 2.

3. Beginning with a vertically oriented block, arrange and sew 10 border units together, rotating them as shown; press. Make two for the top and bottom borders.

Top/bottom border.
Make 2.

16

4. Referring to the photo on page 14 and the diagram below, sew the borders from step 2 to the sides of the quilt. Press the seams toward the border rows. Repeat to sew the borders from step 3 to the top and bottom; press.

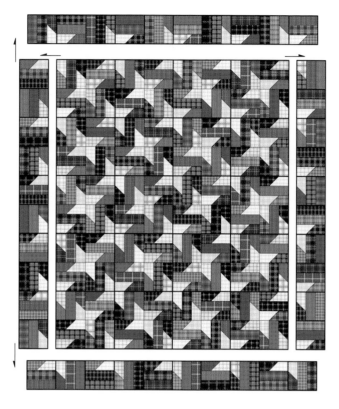

Finishing the Quilt

1. Layer the backing, batting, and quilt top; baste.

2. Use the pearl cotton to tie square knots at the intersection of each block unit to create three-dimensional "barbs."

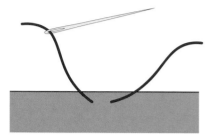

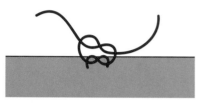

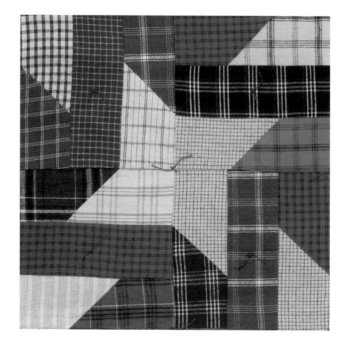

3. Refer to "Making Painless Mitered Binding" on page 12 and use the 2½"-wide strips to bind the quilt edges.

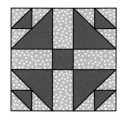

Finished quilt size: 56½" x 66½"
Finished block size: 10" x 10"

Materials

All yardage is based on 42"-wide fabric.

- 4½ yards *total* of assorted light and dark fabrics for blocks and outer border
- ½ yard of contrasting fabric for inner border
- ⅝ yard of fabric for binding
- 4 yards of fabric for backing (vertical seam); 3½ yards (horizontal seam)
- 62" x 72" piece of batting

Cutting

All measurements include ¼"-wide seam allowances. Cut all strips across the width of the fabric.

Fabric	First Cut	Second Cut
Assorted lights and darks	A *total* of 18 strips, 4½" wide	80 half-square triangles in matching sets of 4 (A)
		80 rectangles, 2½" x 4½", in matching sets of 4 (E)
		110 rectangles, 2½" x 4½" (E)
	24 strips, 2½" wide	80 half-square triangles in matching sets of 4 (B)
		240 half-square triangles in matching sets of 12 (C)
		20 squares, 2½" x 2½" (D)
		110 squares, 2½" x 2½" (D)
Contrasting fabric	5 strips, 2½" wide	
Binding	7 strips, 2½" wide	

Scrappy Cutting

When making scrap quilts, I prefer to cut blocks one at a time. This enables me to stay organized and allows the opportunity to plan the color balance throughout the quilt.

Making the Blocks

Refer to page 11 for tips on sewing an accurate ¼" seam allowance. Each block is made from two fabrics.

1. Sew a B half-square triangle and a C half-square triangle together as shown; press. Sew a matching C half-square triangle to adjacent sides of the unit; press. Make four.

Make 4.

2. Sew a matching A half-square triangle to each unit from step 1 as shown; press.

Make 4.

3. Arrange the four units from step 2, a matching D square, and four matching E rectangles as shown. Sew the units and pieces together in vertical rows; press. Sew the rows together to complete the block; press.

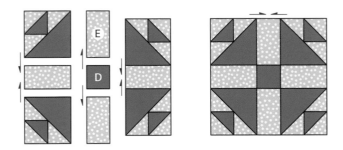

4. Repeat steps 1–3 to make a total of 20 blocks.

Assembling the Quilt

1. Arrange the blocks into five horizontal rows of four blocks each as shown in the assembly diagram. Sew the blocks together into rows; press. Sew the rows together; press.

Assembly diagram

2. Sew the 2½"-wide contrasting strips end to end to make one continuous strip. From this long strip, cut two strips, 2½" x 54½", for the side borders, and two strips, 2½" x 40½", for the top and bottom borders. Sew the appropriate borders to the sides and then to the top and bottom of the quilt top. Press the seams toward the border.

3. Sew a D square and an E rectangle together as shown; press. Make 110.

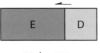

Make 110.

20

4. Arrange and sew 22 units from step 3 together to make a row, rotating the units as shown; press. Make two rows and sew them to the top and bottom of the quilt. Press the seams toward the inner border.

Make 2.

5. Repeat step 4, using 33 remaining units each from step 3 to make the side borders; press. Sew the borders to the sides of the quilt; press.

Make 2.

Finishing the Quilt

1. Layer the backing, batting, and quilt top; baste.

2. Hand or machine quilt as desired.

3. Refer to "Making Painless Mitered Binding" on page 12 and use the 2½"-wide strips to bind the quilt edges.

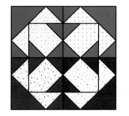

Finished quilt size: 48½" x 48½"
Finished block size: 6" x 6"

Materials

Yardage is based on 42"-wide fabric.

- 2⅛ yards *total* of assorted dark blue fabrics for blocks
- 2⅛ yards *total* of assorted light fabrics for blocks
- ½ yard of fabric for binding
- 3 yards of fabric for backing
- 54" x 54" piece of batting

Cutting

All measurements include ¼"-wide seam allowances. Cut all strips across the width of the fabric.

Fabric	First Cut	Second Cut
Assorted dark blues	A *total* of 7 strips, 4½" wide	28 squares, 4½" x 4½" (A)
		36 half-square triangles (E)
	A *total* of 14 strips, 2½" wide	56 quarter-square triangles in matching pairs (B)
		108 squares, 2½" x 2½", in matching sets of 3 (C)
		72 half-square triangles in matching pairs (D)
Assorted lights	A *total* of 7 strips, 4½" wide	36 squares, 4½" x 4½" (A)
		28 half-square triangles (E)
	A *total* of 15 strips, 2½" wide	72 quarter-square triangles in matching pairs (B)
		84 squares, 2½" x 2½", in matching sets of 3 (C)
		56 half-square triangles in matching pairs (D)
Binding	6 strips, 2½" wide	

Making the Blocks

Refer to page 11 for tips on sewing an accurate ¼" seam allowance. You will make a total of 64 blocks for this quilt in two variations. For 36 blocks, the T motif is light and the background is dark blue (block 1). For 28 blocks, the T motif is dark blue and the background is light (block 2). Each block is made from two fabrics: one light and one dark blue.

Block 1

1. Referring to "Making Flippy Corners" on page 11 and with right sides together, align matching dark C squares to opposite corners of one light A square as shown. Sew, trim, and press. Repeat to sew a matching C square to one remaining corner.

2. Sew a matching dark D half-square triangle to a matching light B quarter-square triangle as shown; press. Make one of each.

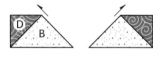

Make 1 of each.

3. Sew the units from step 2 to the unit from step 1 as shown; press. Sew one matching E half-square triangle to the unit to complete the block; press.

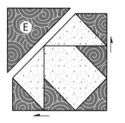

Block 1

4. Repeat steps 1–3 to make a total of 36 of block 1.

Block 2

Reversing the dark blue and light pieces, repeat "Block 1," steps 1–3, to make 28 of block 2.

Block 2

Assembling the Quilt

1. Arrange and sew four of block 1 together, rotating the blocks as shown; press. Make nine.

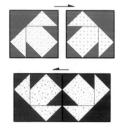
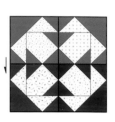

Make 9.

2. Arrange the units from step 1 into three horizontal rows of three units each as shown in the assembly diagram on page 25. Sew the units together into rows; press. Sew the rows together; press.

3. Arrange and sew six of block 2 together, rotating the blocks as shown; press. Make two rows and sew them to the sides of the quilt. Press the seams toward the rows.

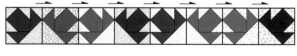

Make 2.

4. Arrange and sew together eight of block 2, rotating the blocks as shown; press. Make two rows and sew them to the top and bottom; press.

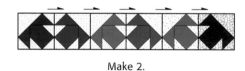

Make 2.

Finishing the Quilt

1. Layer the backing, batting, and quilt top; baste.

2. Hand or machine quilt as desired.

3. Refer to "Making Painless Mitered Binding" on page 12 and use the 2½"-wide strips to bind the quilt edges.

Assembly diagram

Finished quilt size: 72½" x 100½"
Finished block size: 14" x 14"

Materials

Yardage is based on 42"-wide fabric.

- 3 yards of focus print for blocks and outer border
- ⅞ yard *each* of 6 assorted fabrics for blocks
- ⅞ yard of fabric for binding
- 6 yards of fabric for backing (vertical seam)
- 78" x 106" piece of batting

Cutting

All measurements include ¼"-wide seam allowances. Cut all strips across the width of the fabric.

Fabric	First Cut
Focus print	11 strips, 2½" wide
	8 strips, 8½" wide, for borders
Each assorted fabric	11 strips, 2½" wide
Binding	10 strips, 2½" wide

Making the Blocks

Refer to page 11 for tips on sewing an accurate ¼" seam allowance. Before beginning, arrange one of each assorted-color strip and one 2½"-wide focus fabric strip in the order you would like them to appear in your quilt. Cut a small scrap of each fabric from the remaining yardage. Tape the scraps in order onto a sheet of paper, numbering the scraps 1 through 7 as shown. (The sample quilt uses the focus fabric strip in position 7.)

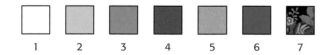

1. Arrange one of each assorted-color strip and the focus fabric strip, following the order on your reference sheet. Sew the strips together along the long edges to make a strip set as shown; press. Make 11 strip sets.

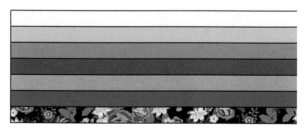

Make 11 strip sets.

2. With right sides together and long raw edges aligned, sew the bottom strip to the top strip in each strip set to make a tube; press. Subcut the tubes into 168 segments, 2½" wide.

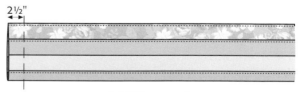

Cut 168 segments.

27

3. Using the segments from step 2, remove the stitches between fabrics 1 and 2 and open up the tube. Make 24. Repeat, using another 24 segments, but this time remove the stitches between fabrics 2 and 3. Continue with the remaining segments, removing the stitches between fabrics 3 and 4, 4 and 5, 5 and 6, and 6 and 7. Make 24 each. Arrange the strips so that the first fabric in the first strip is 1, the first fabric in the second strip is 2, the first fabric in the third strip is 3, and so on, matching the order of your reference sheet. You will have seven stacks, each containing 24 identical strips.

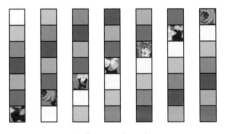

Make 24 of each.

4. Arrange and sew one strip from each stack in order as shown, re-pressing the seams as needed so they nest for accuracy. Make 24.

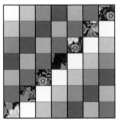

Make 24.

Assembling the Quilt

This is a versatile block and it offers countless design opportunities. Refer to the assembly diagram at right, select a design option from those shown on page 29, or devise a setting of your own, rotating the blocks as necessary to achieve the desired layout.

1. Sew the blocks together into groups of four as shown in the diagram for the layout you have chosen; press. Make six large blocks. Sew the large blocks together into horizontal rows; press. Sew the rows together; press.

2. Sew the 8½"-wide strips end to end to make one continuous strip. From this long strip, cut two strips, 8½" x 84½", for the side borders, and two strips, 8½" x 72½", for the top and bottom borders. Sew the appropriate borders to the sides, top, and bottom of the quilt. Press the seams toward the border.

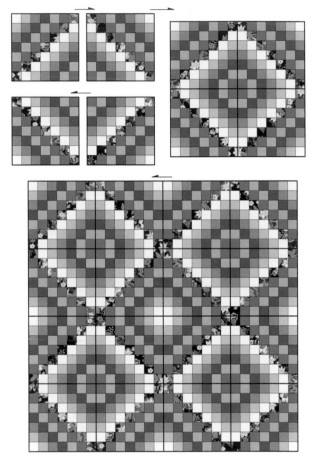

Assembly diagram

Finishing the Quilt

1. Layer the backing, batting, and quilt top; baste.

2. Hand or machine quilt as desired.

3. Refer to "Making Painless Mitered Binding" on page 12 and use the 2½"-wide strips to bind the quilt edges.

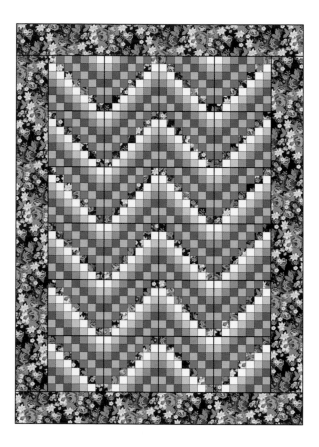

Finished quilt size: 70½" x 70½"
Finished block size: 8" x 8"

Materials

Yardage is based on 42"-wide fabric.

- 4 yards *total* of assorted dark floral prints for blocks and sashing
- 1⅜ yards of light fabric for blocks and sashing
- 1 yard of accent fabric for blocks
- ⅔ yard of fabric for binding
- 4¼ yards of fabric for backing
- 76" x 76" piece of batting

Cutting

All measurements include ¼"-wide seam allowances. Cut all strips across the width of the fabric.

Fabric	First Cut	Second Cut
Assorted dark floral prints	A *total* of 54 strips, 2½" wide	100 rectangles, 2½" x 8½" (D)
		128 rectangles, 2½" x 6½" (C)
		64 rectangles, 2½" x 4½" (B)
		9 squares, 2½" x 2½" (G)
Light	10 strips, 4½" wide	64 squares, 4½" x 4½" (A)
		24 rectangles, 2½" x 4½" (F)
Accent	12 strips, 2½" wide	192 squares, 2½" x 2½" (E)
Binding	8 strips, 2½" wide	

Making the Blocks

Refer to page 11 for tips on sewing an accurate ¼" seam allowance.

1. Referring to "Making Flippy Corners" on page 11 and with right sides together, align a 2½" E square on one corner of each A square as shown. Sew, trim, and press. Make 64.

Make 64.

2. Align and sew an E square onto one end of 64 C and 64 D rectangles, making sure to position the squares as shown; trim and press.

Make 64 of each.

3. Sew a B rectangle to the top edge of each unit from step 1 as shown; press. Sew one E/C unit from step 2 to the left side; press. Make 64.

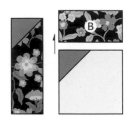

Make 64.

4. Sew a C rectangle to the top edge of each unit from step 3 as shown; press. Sew one E/D unit from step 2 to the left side; press. Make 64.

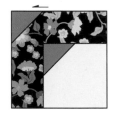

Make 64.

5. Arrange 16 blocks from step 4 in four rows of four blocks each, rotating them as shown. Sew the blocks into rows; press. Sew the rows together; press. Make four.

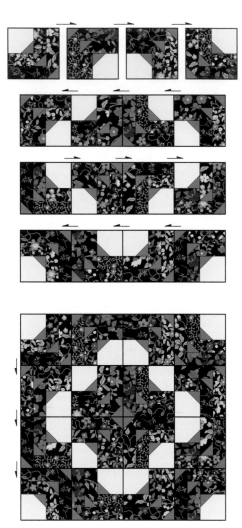

Make 4.

Assembling the Quilt

1. Arrange and sew two F rectangles and three D rectangles together as shown to make a sashing unit; press. Make 12.

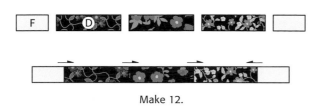

Make 12.

2. Arrange and sew three G squares and two sashing units from step 1 together as shown; press. Make three.

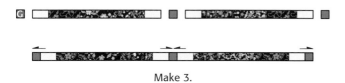

Make 3.

3. Arrange and sew three sashing units from step 1 and two blocks together as shown; press. Make two.

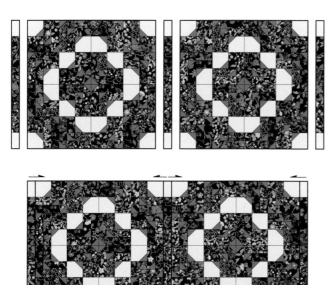

Make 2.

4. Arrange the rows from steps 2 and 3, alternating them as shown in the assembly diagram. Sew the rows together; press.

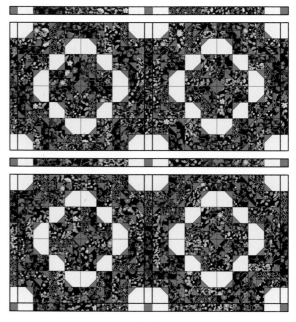

Assembly diagram

Finishing the Quilt

1. Layer the backing, batting, and quilt top; baste.

2. Hand or machine quilt as desired.

3. Refer to "Making Painless Mitered Binding" on page 12 and use the 2½"-wide strips to bind the quilt edges.

Finished quilt size: 32½" x 32½"
Finished block size: 8" x 8"

Materials

Yardage is based on 42"-wide fabric.

- 1 yard *total* of assorted dark floral prints for blocks
- ⅓ yard of light fabric for blocks
- ⅓ yard of accent fabric for blocks
- ⅜ yard of fabric for binding
- 1⅛ yards of fabric for backing
- 38" x 38" piece of batting

Cutting

All measurements include ¼"-wide seam allowances. Cut all strips across the width of the fabric.

Fabric	First Cut	Second Cut
Assorted dark floral prints	A *total* of 12 strips, 2½" wide	16 rectangles, 2½" x 8½" (D)
		32 rectangles, 2½" x 6½" (C)
		16 rectangles, 2½" x 4½" (B)
Light	2 strips, 4½" wide	16 squares, 4½" x 4½" (A)
Accent	3 strips, 2½" wide	48 squares, 2½" x 2½" (E)
Binding	4 strips, 2½" wide	

Making the Table Topper

Refer to page 11 for tips on sewing an accurate ¼" seam allowance.

1. Refer to "Making the Blocks," steps 1–4, on pages 31–32 of "Split the Difference" to make 16 blocks as shown.

Make 16.

2. Arrange and sew four blocks from step 1 in two rows of two blocks each as shown; press. Sew the rows together; press. Make four.

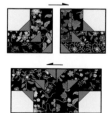 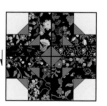

Make 4.

3. Arrange and sew four blocks from step 2 in two rows of two blocks each as shown; press. Sew the rows together; press.

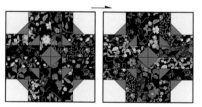

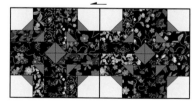

Finishing the Quilt

1. Layer the backing, batting, and quilt top; baste.

2. Hand or machine quilt as desired.

3. Refer to "Making Painless Mitered Binding" on page 12 and use the 2½"-wide strips to bind the quilt edges.

Finished size: 32½" x 32½"

Materials

Yardage is based on 42"-wide fabric.

- 1 yard of light fabric for block
- ¾ yard of dark green fabric for block and border
- ¾ yard of brown floral for block and border
- ¼ yard of red fabric for block
- ⅜ yard of fabric for binding
- 1⅛ yards of fabric for backing
- 38" x 38" piece of batting

Cutting

All measurements include ¼"-wide seam allowances. Cut all strips across the width of the fabric.

Fabric	First Cut	Second Cut
Light	2 strips, 4½" wide	4 squares, 4½" x 4½" (A)
		4 half-square triangles (E)
		4 rectangles, 4½" x 6½" (G)
	8 strips, 2½" wide	64 squares, 2½" x 2½" (B)
		16 rectangles, 2½" x 4½" (C)
		16 half-square triangles (D)
		4 rectangles, 2½" x 6½" (H)
Brown floral	7 strips, 2½" wide	12 squares, 2½" x 2½" (B)
		48 rectangles, 2½" x 4½" (C)
		1 square, 4½" x 4½" (A)
Dark green	1 strip, 4½" wide	4 squares, 4½" x 4½" (A)
	7 strips, 2½" wide	56 squares, 2½" x 2½" (B)
		16 rectangles, 2½" x 4½" (C)
		8 half-square triangles (D)
Red	1 strip, 4½" wide	4 half-square triangles (E)
	1 strip, 2½" wide	4 quarter-square triangles (F)
Binding	4 strips, 2½" wide	

Making the Center Block

Refer to page 11 for tips on sewing an accurate ¼" seam allowance.

1. Referring to "Making Flippy Corners" on page 11 and with right sides together, align a dark green B square on one end of one light C rectangle, and a floral B square on the other end of the rectangle as shown. Sew, trim, and press. Make four of each.

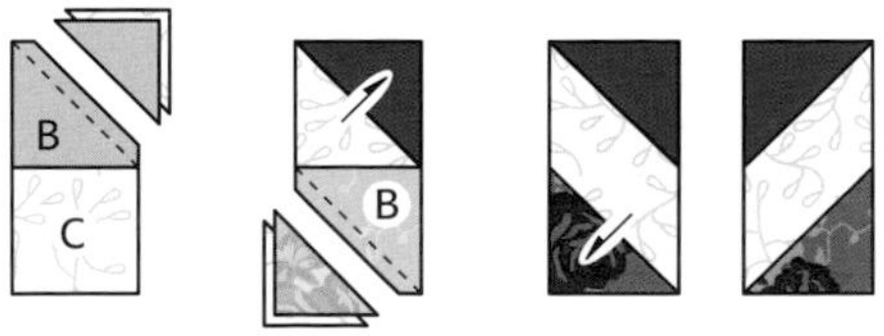

Make 4 of each.

2. Sew one of each unit from step 1 together as shown; press. Make four.

Make 4.

3. Sew a light E half-square triangle and a red E half-square triangle together as shown; press. Make four.

Make 4.

4. Arrange the units from steps 2 and 3 and the floral A square in three rows as shown. Sew the units and square into rows; press. Sew the rows together; press.

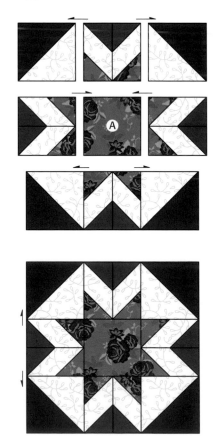

Center block

Assembling the Large Star Block

Refer to "Making the Large Star Blocks," steps 1–10, on pages 93–94 of "Feathered Foursome" and the diagram below to make one large Star block. Use a red F quarter-square triangle in step 1 and the center block you've just completed for center blocks 1–4 in step 10.

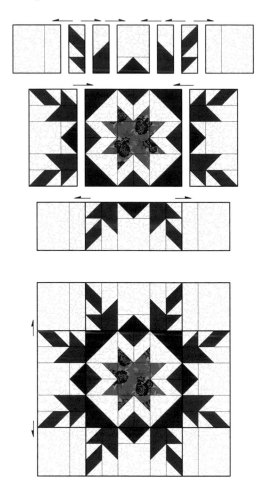

Adding the Border

1. Referring to "Making Flippy Corners" on page 11 and with right sides together, align a dark B square on one end of a floral C rectangle, and a light green B square on the other end of the rectangle as shown. Sew, trim, and press. Make 24 of each.

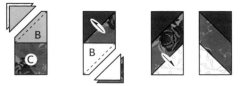

Make 24 of each.

2. Sew one of each unit from step 1 together as shown; press. Make 24.

Make 24.

3. Referring to "Making Flippy Corners," align a floral B square with one corner of each dark green A square as shown. Sew, trim, and press. Make four.

4. Sew six units from step 2 together as shown; press. Make four of these pieced-border units. Sew a unit to opposite sides of the quilt, carefully orienting the units as shown in the assembly diagram at right. Press the seams toward the pieced borders.

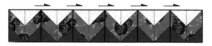

Make 4.

5. Sew a unit from step 3 to opposite ends of each remaining unit from step 4 as shown; press. Make two and sew them to the top and bottom of the quilt; press.

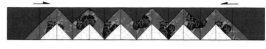

Make 2.

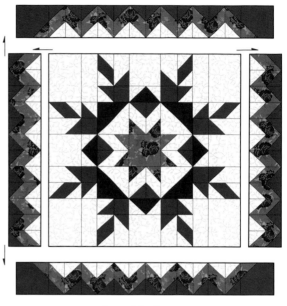

Assembly diagram

Finishing the Quilt

1. Layer the backing, batting, and quilt top; baste.

2. Hand or machine quilt as desired.

3. Refer to "Making Painless Mitered Binding" on page 12 and use the 2½"-wide strips to bind the quilt edges.

Finished quilt size: 44½" x 60½"
Finished block size: 8" x 8"

Materials

All yardage is based on 42"-wide fabric.

- 1½ yards *total* of assorted prints for block backgrounds
- 1⅛ yards *total* of assorted prints for anvil motif in blocks
- ⅞ yard of focus print for outer border
- ⅜ yard *total* of assorted light prints for pieced border
- ⅜ yard *total* of assorted dark prints for pieced border
- ½ yard of fabric for binding
- 3¾ yards of fabric for backing (vertical seam); 2⅞ yards (horizontal seam)
- 50" x 66" piece of batting

Cutting

All measurements include ¼"-wide seam allowances. Cut all strips across the width of the fabric.

Fabric	First Cut
Assorted anvil motif prints	24 squares, 4½" x 4½" (A)
	192 half-square triangles in matching sets of 8 (B)
Assorted background prints	48 half-square triangles in matching pairs (E)
	96 half-square triangles in matching sets of 4 (C)
	48 squares, 2½" x 2½", in matching pairs (D)
Assorted lights for pieced border	84 half-square triangles (F)
Assorted darks for pieced border	84 half-square triangles (G)
Focus print	6 strips, 4½" wide
Binding	6 strips, 2½" wide

Making the Blocks

Refer to page 11 for tips on sewing an accurate ¼" seam allowance. Each block uses two fabrics: one for the anvil motif and one for the background.

1. Sew an anvil-print B half-square triangle and a background C half-square triangle together as shown; press. Make four.

Make 4.

41

2. Sew an anvil-print B half-square triangle to one unit from step 1; press. Make two. Sew a unit to the top and bottom of one anvil-print A square as shown; press.

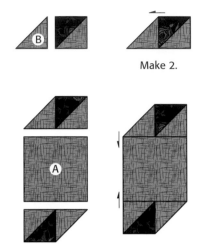

Make 2.

3. Sew a remaining unit from step 1 between an anvil-print B half-square triangle and a background D square as shown; press. Make two.

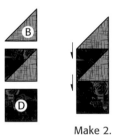

Make 2.

4. Sew a unit from step 3 to the sides of the unit from step 2 as shown; press.

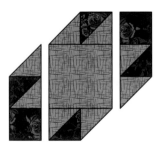
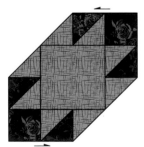

5. Sew the unit from step 4 between two background E half-square triangles as shown; press.

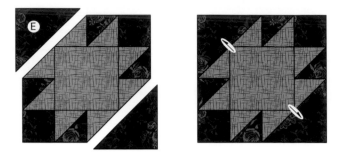

6. Repeat steps 1–5 to make a total of 24 blocks.

Assembling the Quilt

1. Arrange the blocks in six horizontal rows of four blocks each, rotating the blocks as shown in the assembly diagram. Sew the blocks together into rows; press. Sew the rows together; press.

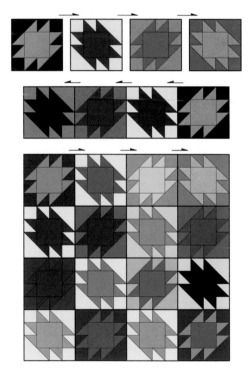

Assembly diagram

2. Sew an assorted light F half-square triangle and an assorted dark G half-square triangle together as shown; press. Make 84.

Make 84.

3. Sew 24 units from step 2 together to make a pieced-border unit, changing direction in the middle of the border as shown; press. Make two and sew them to the sides of the quilt as shown in the diagram at right. Press the seams toward the pieced borders.

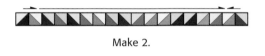

Make 2.

4. Sew 18 remaining units from step 2 together, taking care to turn the end triangles and change direction in the middle of the border as shown. Make two and sew them to the top and bottom of the quilt; press.

Make 2.

5. Sew the 4½"-wide focus-print strips end to end to make one continuous strip. From this long strip, cut two strips, 4½" x 52½", for the side borders, and two strips, 4½" x 44½", for the top and bottom borders. Sew the appropriate borders to the sides and then to the top and bottom of the quilt top. Press the seams toward the newly added border.

Finishing the Quilt

1. Layer the backing, batting, and quilt top; baste.

2. Hand or machine quilt as desired.

3. Refer to "Making Painless Mitered Binding" on page 12 and use the 2½"-wide strips to bind the quilt edges.

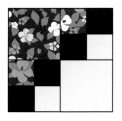

Finished quilt size: 56½" x 72½"
Finished block size: 8" x 8"

Materials

Yardage is based on 42"-wide fabric.

- 3 yards of focus print for blocks, border, and binding
- 1⅓ yards of light fabric for blocks
- 1 yard of contrasting accent fabric for blocks
- 4 yards of fabric for backing (vertical seam); 3⅛ yards (horizontal seam)
- 62" x 78" piece of batting

Cutting

All measurements include ¼"-wide seam allowances. Cut all strips across the width of the fabric.

Fabric	First Cut	Second Cut
Focus print	6 strips, 4½" wide	48 squares, 4½" x 4½" (A)
	7 strips, 4½" wide, for border	
	6 strips, 2½" wide (B)	
	7 strips, 2½" wide, for binding	
Light	6 strips, 4½" wide	48 squares, 4½" x 4½" (D)
	6 strips, 2½" wide (C)	
Accent	12 strips, 2½" wide (E)	

Making the Blocks

Refer to page 11 for tips on sewing an accurate ¼" seam allowance.

1. Sew a C strip and an E strip together along the long edges to make a strip set; press. Make six strip sets. Subcut the strip sets into 96 segments, 2½" wide.

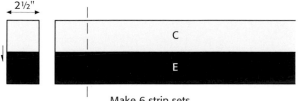

Make 6 strip sets.
Cut 96 segments.

2. Sew a B strip and an E strip together along the long edges to make a strip set; press. Make six strip sets. Subcut the strip sets into 96 segments, 2½" wide.

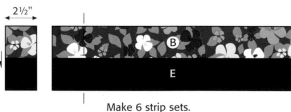

Make 6 strip sets.
Cut 96 segments.

3. Sew together a segment each from steps 1 and 2 to make a four-patch unit; press. Make 96.

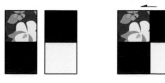

Make 96.

4. Arrange two units from step 3 and an A and D square as shown. Sew the units and squares together to complete the block; press. Make 48.

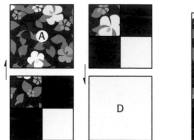 

Make 48.

Assembling the Quilt

1. Arrange the blocks in eight horizontal rows of six blocks each, orienting the blocks as shown in the assembly diagram. Sew the blocks together into rows; press. Sew the rows together; press.

2. Sew the 4½"-wide focus-print strips end to end to make one continuous strip. From this long strip, cut two strips, 4½" x 64½", for the side borders, and two strips, 4½" x 56½", for the top and bottom borders. Sew the appropriate borders to the sides and then to the top and bottom of the quilt top. Press the seams toward the border.

Finishing the Quilt

1. Layer the backing, batting, and quilt top; baste.

2. Hand or machine quilt as desired.

3. Refer to "Making Painless Mitered Binding" on page 12 and use the remaining 2½"-wide focus-print strips to bind the quilt edges.

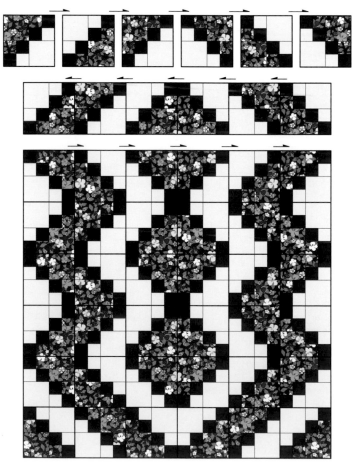

Assembly diagram

Materials

Yardage is based on 42"-wide fabric.

- 1⅞ yards of focus print for Chain blocks and binding
- 1⅜ yards of light fabric for Chain and Spinning Star blocks
- 1 yard of brown accent fabric for Chain blocks
- 1 yard *total* of assorted blue fabrics for Spinning Star blocks
- 1 yard *total* of assorted green fabrics for Spinning Star blocks
- 1 yard of medium tan fabric for Chain blocks and corner squares
- 4⅞ yards of fabric for backing (vertical seam); 3 yards (horizontal seam)
- 54" x 86" piece of batting

 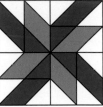

Finished quilt size: 48½" x 80½"
Finished block size: 8" x 8"

Cutting

All measurements include ¼"-wide seam allowances. Cut all strips across the width of the fabric.

Fabric	First Cut	Second Cut
Focus print	6 strips, 4½" wide	44 squares, 4½" x 4½" (B)
	6 strips, 2½" wide (C)	
	7 strips, 2½"wide, for binding	
Medium tan	3 strips, 4½" wide	24 squares, 4½" x 4½" (A)
	3 strips, 2½" wide (D)	
	1 strip, 8½" wide	4 squares, 8½" x 8½" (L)
Brown accent	12 strips, 2½" wide (E)	
Light	3 strips, 4½" wide	20 squares, 4½" x 4½" (G)
	9 strips, 2½" wide	144 squares, 2½"x 2½" (I)
	3 strips, 2½" wide (F)	
Assorted blues	A *total* of 12 strips, 2½" wide	From *each* strip, cut 4 rectangles, 2½" x 4½" (H) and 4 squares, 2½" x 2½" (J).
Assorted greens	A *total* of 12 strips, 2½" wide	From *each* strip, cut 4 rectangles, 2½" x 4½" (K).

Making the Blocks

Refer to page 11 for tips on sewing an accurate ¼" seam allowance. You will make a total of 56 blocks for this quilt: 44 Chain blocks (in two variations) and 12 Spinning Star blocks.

Chain Blocks

The Chain block appears in two different color combinations: Chain block 1 and Chain block 2. You will make 24 of Chain block 1 (with medium tan background) and 20 of Chain block 2 (with light background).

Chain block 1

Chain block 2

1. Sew a C strip and an E strip together along the long edges to make a strip set; press. Make six strip sets. Subcut the strip sets into 88 segments, 2½" wide.

2½"
Make 6 strip sets.
Cut 88 segments.

2. Sew a D strip and an E strip together along the long edges to make a strip set; press. Make three strip sets. Subcut the strip sets into 48 segments, 2½" wide.

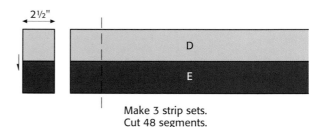
2½"
D
E
Make 3 strip sets.
Cut 48 segments.

3. Sew an E strip and an F strip together along the long edges to make a strip set; press. Make three strip sets. Subcut the strip sets into 40 segments, 2½" wide.

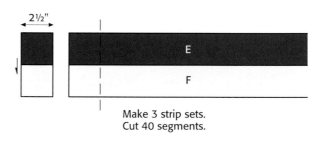
2½"
E
F
Make 3 strip sets.
Cut 40 segments.

4. Sew together a segment each from steps 1 and 2 to make a four-patch unit; press. Make 48 and label them unit 1. Repeat, using the segments from steps 1 and 3. Make 40 and label them unit 2.

Unit 1.
Make 48.

Unit 2.
Make 40.

5. Arrange two of unit 1 from step 4 and an A and B square as shown. Sew the units and squares together to complete the block; press. Make 24 and label them Chain block 1. Repeat, using two of unit 2 from step 4 and the G and remaining B squares. Make 20 and label them Chain block 2.

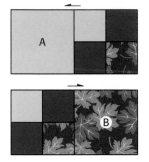

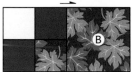

Chain block 1.
Make 24.

Chain block 2.
Make 20.

Spinning Star Blocks

While all the Spinning Star blocks use the same light fabric throughout, each block uses a different combination of one blue fabric and one green fabric for a scrappy look.

1. Referring to "Making Flippy Corners" on page 11 and with right sides together, align an I square on each end of an H rectangle as shown. Sew, trim, and press. Make 48 in matching sets of four.

Make 48
in matching
sets of 4.

2. Repeat step 1, using I squares, J squares, and K rectangles as shown. Make 48 in matching sets of four.

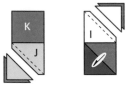

Make 48
in matching
sets of 4.

3. Sew a unit from step 1 to a color-matched unit from step 2 as shown; press. Make 48 in matching sets of four.

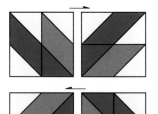

Make 48
in matching
sets of 4.

4. Arrange four matching units from step 3 as shown. Sew the units together to complete the block; press. Make 12.

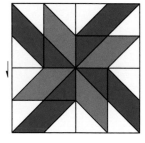

Make 12.

Assembling the Quilt

Arrange the Chain 1 and 2 blocks, the Spinning Star blocks, and four L squares in 10 horizontal rows of six blocks and squares each, orienting the Chain blocks as shown in the assembly diagram below. Sew the blocks and squares together into rows; press. Sew the rows together; press.

Finishing the Quilt

1. Layer the backing, batting, and quilt top; baste.

2. Hand or machine quilt as desired.

3. Refer to "Making Painless Mitered Binding" on page 12 and use the remaining 2½"-wide focus-print strips to bind the quilt edges.

Assembly diagram

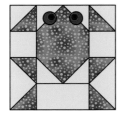

Finished quilt size: 52½" x 52½"
Finished block size: 8" x 8"

Materials

Yardage is based on 42"-wide fabric unless noted otherwise.

- 2¼ yards of light green fabric for blocks and inner pieced border
- 1 yard of dark green fabric for inner pieced border and outer border
- 1 yard of lime green fabric for splash appliqués and binding
- ¼ yard of large polka-dot print for eye appliqués
- 12 fat eighths (9" x 22") of assorted bright fabrics for blocks
- 3¼ yards of fabric for backing
- 58" x 58" piece of batting
- ½ yard of fusible web

Cutting

All measurements include ¼"-wide seam allowances. Cut all strips across the width of the fabric.

Fabric	First Cut	Second Cut
Each bright	1 strip, 4½" wide	1 rectangle, 4½" x 6½" (A)
	1 strip, 2½" wide	4 squares, 2½" x 2½" (E)
		2 half-square triangles (D)
Light green	4 strips, 8½" wide	13 squares, 8½" x 8½" (I)
	3 strips, 4½"wide	36 rectangles, 2½" x 4½" (F)
	10 strips, 2½" wide	72 squares, 2½" x 2½"(B)
		24 half-square triangles (C)
		40 quarter-square triangles (G)
Dark green	3 strips, 2½" wide	44 quarter-square triangles (H)
	5 strips, 4½" wide	
Lime green	6 strips, 2½" wide, for binding	

Making the Blocks

Refer to page 11 for tips on sewing an accurate ¼" seam allowance. While all the blocks use the same light green fabric for the background, each block uses a different bright fabric for the frog.

1. Referring to "Making Flippy Corners" on page 11 and with right sides together, align B squares on opposite corners of an A rectangle as shown. Sew, trim, and press. Repeat to sew B squares to the remaining corners.

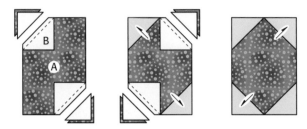

2. Sew a C half-square triangle and a D half-square triangle together as shown; press. Make two matching units.

Make 2.

3. Referring to "Making Flippy Corners" and with right sides together, align an E square on one end of an F rectangle as shown. Sew, trim, and press. Repeat to sew a matching E square to the opposite end. Make two matching units.

Make 2.

4. Arrange the units from steps 1–3, two B squares, and an F rectangle as shown. Sew the units and pieces together in vertical rows; press. Sew the rows together to complete the block; press.

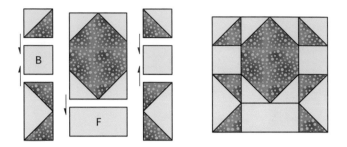

5. Repeat steps 1–4 to make a total of 12 blocks.

Adding the Eye Appliqués

I used polka-dot fabric and the following method to hand appliqué two eyeballs to each block as shown. Alternatively, you can iron the eyeballs into place, using fusible web, and finish the raw edges with decorative stitching. Read and follow the manufacturer's instructions for working with the fusible product.

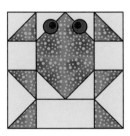

1. Trace around a small coin, such as a dime, onto the dull side of a small piece of freezer paper. Cut out the circle directly on the traced line.

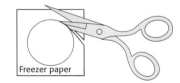

Freezer paper

2. Selectively position the paper template, shiny side down, to take advantage of a dot on the right side of the polka-dot fabric; press.

3. Trim around the freezer-paper template, adding ⅛" to ¼" for the turn-under seam allowance.

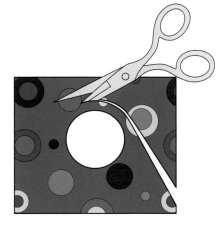

4. Position the appliqué piece on the Frog block, paper side up, and pin it in place. Using the edge of the freezer paper as a guide, use the point of your needle to turn under the seam allowance of the fabric, and sew the shape in place with small, invisible stitches. Remove the freezer paper. Repeat to add two eye appliqués to each Frog block.

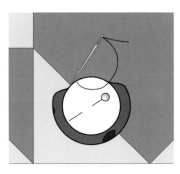

Assembling the Quilt

1. Arrange the blocks and I squares into five horizontal rows of five blocks each, alternating the blocks and squares and turning the blocks as shown in the assembly diagram. Sew the blocks and squares together into rows; press. Sew the rows together; press.

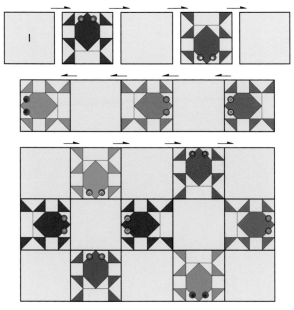

Assembly diagram

2. Sew 10 G quarter-square triangles and 9 H quarter-square triangles together to make an inner-border row as shown; press. Make four.

Make 4.

3. Sew two remaining H quarter-square triangles together to make a corner unit as shown; press. Make four.

Make 4.

4. Sew a border row from step 2 to the sides, top, and bottom of the quilt. Press the seams toward the border row. Sew a unit from step 3 to each corner. Press the seams toward the corner units.

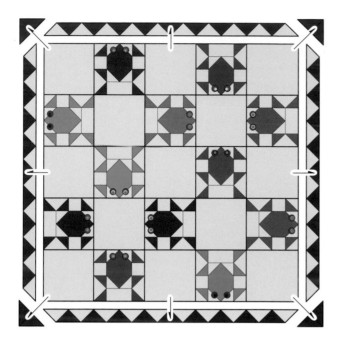

5. Sew the 4½"-wide dark green strips end to end to make one continuous strip. From this long strip, cut two strips, 4½" x 44½", for the side outer borders, and two strips, 4½" x 52½", for the top and bottom outer borders. Sew the appropriate borders to the sides and then to the top and bottom of the quilt top. Press the seams toward the border.

6. Use the remaining lime green fabric, the fusible web, and the patterns below to prepare 12 large splash appliqués and 8 small splash appliqués (4 and 4 reversed) for fusing. Read and follow the manufacturer's instructions for working with the fusible product.

7. Refer to the quilt photo on page 52 to position and fuse the appliqués in place. Finish the raw edges with your favorite machine stitch.

Finishing the Quilt

1. Layer the backing, batting, and quilt top; baste.

2. Hand or machine quilt as desired.

3. Refer to "Making Painless Mitered Binding" on page 12 and use the 2½"-wide lime green strips to bind the quilt edges.

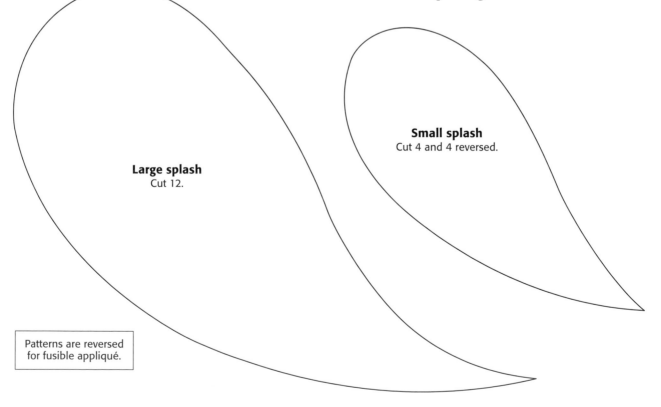

Large splash
Cut 12.

Small splash
Cut 4 and 4 reversed.

Patterns are reversed for fusible appliqué.

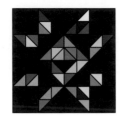

Finished quilt size: 46½" x 46½"
Finished block size: 16" x 16"

Materials

Yardage is based on 42"-wide fabric.

- 1⅜ yards of dark solid for blocks and outer border
- ¾ yard *total* of bright solids for blocks and inner corner squares
- ⅔ yard of teal solid for sashing, inner border, and outer-border corner squares
- ½ yard of fabric for binding
- 2⅞ yards of fabric for backing
- 52" x 52" piece of batting

Cutting

All measurements include ¼"-wide seam allowances. Cut all strips across the width of the fabric.

Fabric	First Cut	Second Cut
Brights	A *total* of 9 strips, 2½" wide	192 half-square triangles (A)
		5 squares, 2½" x 2½" (E)
Dark	10 strips, 4½" wide	48 half-square triangles (B)
		16 squares, 4½" x 4½" (C)
		4 strips, 4½" x 38½"
Teal	6 strips, 2½" wide	4 strips, 2½" x 16½" (D)
		4 strips, 2½" x 34½"
	1 strip, 4½" wide	4 squares, 4½" x 4½" (F)
Binding	5 strips, 2½" wide	

Making the Blocks

Refer to page 11 for tips on sewing an accurate ¼" seam allowance.

1. Sew two assorted A half-square triangles together as shown; press. Sew assorted A half-square triangles to two adjacent sides of the unit; press. Make 48.

Make 48.

2. Sew a B half-square triangle to each unit from step 1 as shown; press. Make 48.

Make 48.

3. Arrange 12 units from step 2 and four C squares as shown. Sew the units and squares together into rows; press. Sew the rows together to complete the block; press. Make four.

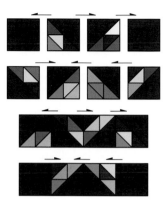

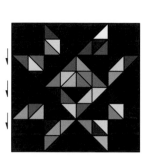

Make 4.

Assembling the Quilt

1. Sew a D strip between two blocks as shown; press. Make two.

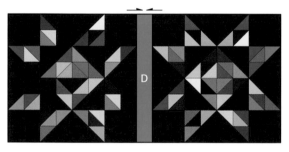

Make 2.

2. Sew an E square between the remaining D strips as shown; press. Sew this strip between the two rows from step 1; press.

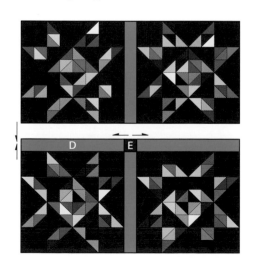

3. Referring to the assembly diagram, sew a 2½" x 34½" inner-border strip to the top and bottom of the quilt. Press the seams toward the strips. Sew a remaining E square to each end of each remaining 2½" x 34½" strip; press. Make two and sew them to the sides; press.

4. Repeat step 3, using the F squares and the 4½" x 38½" strips to add the outer borders. Press the seams toward the outer border.

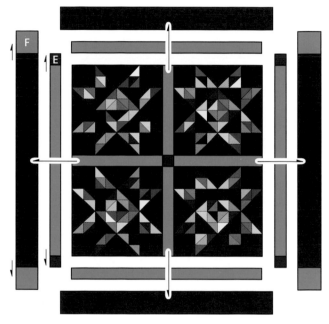

Assembly diagram

Finishing the Quilt

1. Layer the backing, batting, and quilt top; baste.

2. Hand or machine quilt as desired.

3. Refer to "Making Painless Mitered Binding" on page 12 and use the 2½"-wide strips to bind the quilt edges.

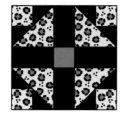

Finished quilt size: 58½" x 74½"
Finished block size: 10" x 10"

Materials

Yardage is based on 42"-wide fabric.

- 4⅝ yards of black fabric for blocks, setting triangles, borders, and binding
- 1⅛ yards *total* of assorted animal prints for blocks and pieced border
- ⅛ yard of accent fabric for blocks
- 4½ yards of fabric for backing (vertical seam); 3⅝ yards (horizontal seam)
- 64" x 80" piece of batting

Cutting

In one of the few exceptions in this book, the inner borders and setting triangles are not cut from 2½" or 4½" strips. All measurements include ¼"-wide seam allowances. Cut all strips across the width of the fabric.

Fabric	First Cut	Second Cut
Black	3 strips, 15⅜" wide	6 squares, 15⅜" x 15⅜"; cut twice diagonally to yield 24 quarter-square triangles (G). You will have 2 triangles left over.
	1 strip, 8" wide	2 squares, 8" x 8"; cut once diagonally to yield 4 half-square triangles (F)
	3 strips, 4½" wide	48 rectangles, 2½" x 4½" (E)
	7 strips, 4½" wide, for outer border	
	8 strips, 2½" wide	96 half-square triangles (B)
		56 squares, 2½" x 2½" (H)
	7 strips, 2½" wide, for binding	
	3 strips, 2¼" wide, for inner border	
	3 strips, 3¼" wide, for inner border	
Animal prints	48 half-square triangles in matching sets of 4 (C)	
	48 squares, 2½" x 2½", in matching sets of 4 (A)	
	56 squares, 2½" x 2½" (I)	
Accent	1 strip, 2½" wide	12 squares, 2½" x 2½" (D)

Making the Blocks

Refer to page 11 for tips on sewing an accurate ¼" seam allowance. While all the blocks use the same black fabric for the background and the same accent fabric for the block center, each block uses a different animal print.

1. Sew a B half-square triangle to adjacent sides of an A square; press. Make four.

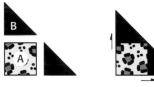

Make 4.

2. Sew a matching C half-square triangle to each unit from step 1 as shown; press. Make four.

Make 4.

3. Arrange the four units from step 2, a D square, and four E rectangles as shown. Sew the units and pieces together in vertical rows; press. Sew the rows together to complete the block; press.

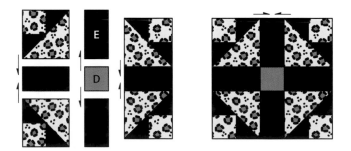

4. Repeat steps 1–3 to make a total of 12 blocks.

Assembling the Quilt

This quilt is assembled in an unusual sequence. You will construct each subsection and then build the quilt from the center out by sewing the subsections as indicated in the assembly diagram on page 63.

1. Arrange the four F half-square triangles, two G quarter-square triangles, and two blocks in diagonal rows as shown; press. Sew the rows and triangles together; press.

2. Sew a G quarter-square triangle to opposite ends of the unit from step 1 as shown; press.

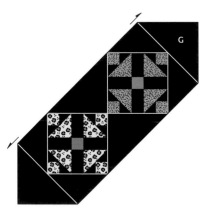

3. Sew a G quarter-square triangle to adjacent sides of a remaining block; press. Make two and sew them to opposite sides of the unit from step 2 as shown; press.

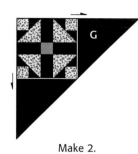

Make 2.

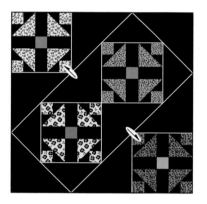

4. Arrange and sew two blocks and three G quarter-square triangles together as shown; press. Make two.

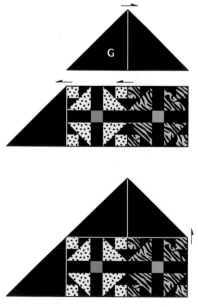

Make 2.

5. Arrange and sew two blocks and four G quarter-square triangles together as shown; press. Make two.

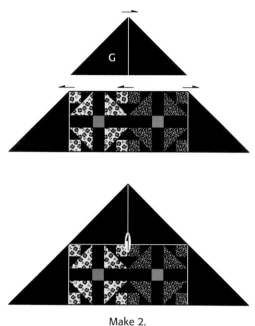

Make 2.

6. Arrange the unit from step 3, the two units from step 4, and the two units from step 5 as shown in the assembly diagram. Sew the units from step 4 to the unit from step 3; press. Add the units from step 5; press.

Assembly diagram

7. Sew the 2¼"-wide strips end to end to make one continuous strip. From this long strip, cut two strips, 2¼" x 57", for the side inner borders. Sew the borders to the sides of the quilt top. Press the seams toward the border.

8. Sew the 3¼"-wide strips end to end to make one continuous strip. From this long strip, cut two strips, 3¼" x 46½", for the top and bottom inner borders. Sew the borders to the top and bottom; press.

9. Arrange and sew 12 H squares and 11 I squares together, alternating them to make a row as shown; press toward the black squares. Make two and sew them to the top and bottom of the quilt. Press the seams toward the inner border.

Make 2.

10. Repeat step 9 using 16 H squares and 17 I squares as shown; press toward the black squares. Make two and sew them to the sides of the quilt.

Make 2.

11. Sew the 4½"-wide strips end to end to make one continuous strip. From this long strip, cut two strips, 4½" x 66½", for the side outer borders, and two strips, 4½" x 58½", for the top and bottom outer borders. Sew the appropriate borders to the sides, and then to the top and bottom of the quilt top. Press the seams toward the border.

Finishing the Quilt

1. Layer the backing, batting, and quilt top; baste.

2. Hand or machine quilt as desired.

3. Refer to "Making Painless Mitered Binding" on page 12 and use the 2½"-wide black strips to bind the quilt edges.

Retreat to the Lake

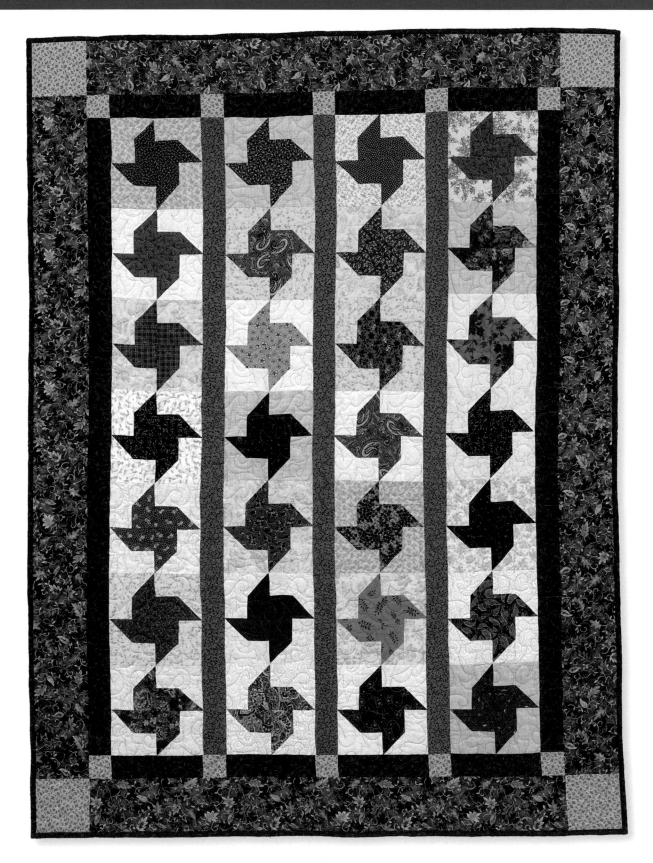

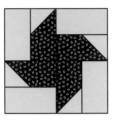

Finished quilt size: 50½" x 68½"
Finished block size: 8" x 8"

Materials

Yardage is based on 42"-wide fabric.

- 1½ yards *total* of assorted light prints for blocks
- 1 yard *total* of assorted medium and dark prints for blocks
- ⅞ yard of focus print for outer border
- ½ yard of tan fabric for sashing strips
- ½ yard of red fabric for inner border
- ¼ yard of gold fabric for sashing and border cornerstones
- ⅝ yard of fabric for binding
- 4⅛ yards of fabric for backing (vertical seam); 3⅛ yards (horizontal seam)
- 56" x 74" piece of batting

Cutting

All measurements include ¼"-wide seam allowances. Cut all strips across the width of the fabric.

Fabric	First Cut	Second Cut
Assorted medium and dark prints	112 rectangles, 2½" x 4½", in matching sets of 4 (A)	
Assorted light prints	112 rectangles, 2½" x 4½", in matching sets of 4 (C)	
	112 squares, 2½" x 2½", in matching sets of 4 (B)	
Tan	5 strips, 2½" wide	
Red	2 strips, 2½" wide	8 strips, 2½" x 8½" (E)
	3 strips, 2½" wide, for inner border	
Gold	1 strip, 4½" wide	4 squares, 4½" x 4½" (F)
	1 strip, 2½" wide	10 squares, 2½" x 2½" (D)
Focus print	6 strips, 4½" wide, for outer border	
Binding	7 strips, 2½" wide	

Making the Blocks

Refer to page 11 for tips on sewing an accurate ¼" seam allowance. Each block is made from two fabrics.

1. Referring to "Making Flippy Corners" on page 11 and with right sides together, align a B square with one end of an A rectangle as shown. Sew, trim, and press. Make 112 in matching sets of four.

Make 112
in matching
sets of 4.

2. Sew a matching C rectangle to each unit from step 1 as shown; press. Make 112.

Make 112.

3. Arrange four matching units from step 2, orienting them as shown. Sew the units together to complete the block; press. Make 28.

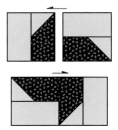
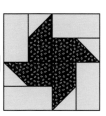

Make 28.

Assembling the Quilt

1. Arrange the blocks into four vertical rows of seven blocks each as shown in the assembly diagram. Sew the blocks together into rows; press.

2. Sew the 2½"-wide tan strips together end to end to make one long strip. From this long strip, cut three sashing strips that measure 2½" x 56½". Repeat, using the 2½"-wide red strips to make two inner-border strips, 2½" x 56½".

3. Arrange the rows from step 1 and the tan and red strips from step 2, alternating them as shown in the assembly diagram. Sew the rows and strips together; press.

4. Arrange and sew five D squares and four E strips together to make a row as shown; press. Make two rows and sew them to the top and bottom of the quilt; press.

Make 2.

5. Sew the 4½"-wide strips end to end to make one continuous strip. From this long strip, cut two strips, 4½" x 60½", for the side borders, and two strips, 4½" x 42½", for the top and bottom borders.

6. Sew the 4½" x 60½" borders to the sides of the quilt. Press the seams toward the outer border. Sew an F square to each end of each 4½" x 42½" strip; press. Make two and sew them to the top and bottom; press the seams toward the strips.

Assembly diagram

Finishing the Quilt

1. Layer the backing, batting, and quilt top; baste.

2. Hand or machine quilt as desired.

3. Refer to "Making Painless Mitered Binding" on page 12 and use the 2½"-wide strips to bind the quilt edges.

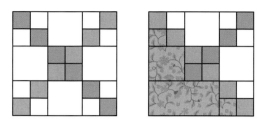

Finished quilt size: 96½" x 108½"
Finished block sizes: 8" x 12" (block 1)
4" x 12" (block 2)
12" x 12" (blocks 3 and 4)

Materials

Yardage is based on 42"-wide fabric.

- 4¾ yards of white fabric for blocks
- 4¼ yards of focus print for blocks, outer border, and binding
- 1¾ yards of light green fabric for blocks
- 1½ yards of light blue fabric for blocks
- ⅞ yard of accent fabric for inner border
- 9½ yards of fabric for backing (vertical seam); 8½ yards (horizontal seam)
- 102" x 114" piece of batting

Cutting

All measurements include ¼"-wide seam allowances. Cut all strips across the width of the fabric.

Fabric	First Cut	Second Cut
White	28 strips, 2½" wide	
	13 strips, 4½" wide	104 squares, 4½" x 4½"
	7 strips, 4½" wide, for strip sets	
Focus print	11 strips, 4½" wide	20 squares, 4½" x 4½"
		29 rectangles, 4½" x 8½"
	11 strips, 4½" wide, for outer border	
	3 strips, 2½" wide	
	11 strips, 2½" wide, for binding	
Light green	22 strips, 2½" wide	
Light blue	19 strips, 2½" wide	
Accent	10 strips, 2½" wide	

Making the Blocks

Refer to page 11 for tips on sewing an accurate ¼" seam allowance. You will make a total of 72 blocks for this quilt in four variations: 18 each of blocks 1 and 2, 16 of block 3, and 20 of block 4.

Blocks 1 and 2

1. Arrange and sew together two 2½"-wide white strips, one 4½"-wide white strip, one light green strip, and one light blue strip along the long edges as shown to make a strip set; press. Make seven strip sets. Subcut five strip sets into a total of 18 segments, 8½" wide. Label the segments block 1.

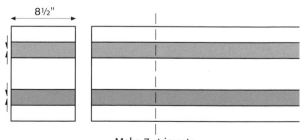

Make 7 strip sets.
Cut 18 segments (Block 1).

2. Subcut the remaining strip sets from step 1 into 18 segments, 4½" wide. Label the segments block 2.

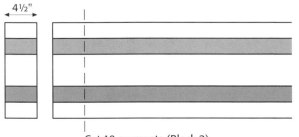

Cut 18 segments (Block 2).

Block 3

1. Sew together a 2½"-wide white strip and a light green strip along the long edges to make a strip set; press. Make four strip sets. Subcut the strip sets into 64 segments, 2½" wide.

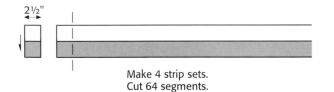

Make 4 strip sets.
Cut 64 segments.

2. Sew together two segments from step 1 as shown to make a four-patch unit; press. Make 32.

Make 32.

3. Repeat steps 1 and 2, using 2½"-wide white strips and light blue strips to make 32 four-patch units as shown.

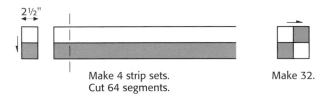

Make 4 strip sets.
Cut 64 segments.

Make 32.

4. Repeat steps 1 and 2, using light blue strips and light green strips. Make two strip sets, cut 32 segments, and make 16 four-patch units.

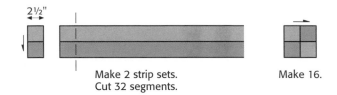

Make 2 strip sets.
Cut 32 segments.

Make 16.

5. Arrange and sew together two units each from steps 2 and 3, one unit from step 4, and four 4½" white squares as shown; press. Make 16 and label them block 3.

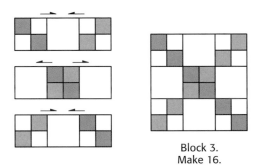

Block 3.
Make 16.

Block 4

1. Sew together a 2½"-wide focus-print strip and a light green strip along the long edges to make a strip set; press. Make three strip sets. Subcut the strip sets into 40 segments, 2½" wide. Repeat, using 2½"-wide white strips and light green strips as shown.

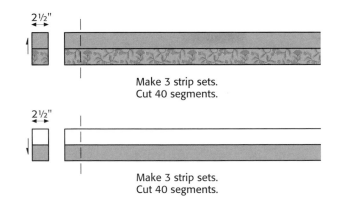

Make 3 strip sets.
Cut 40 segments.

Make 3 strip sets.
Cut 40 segments.

2. Sew together one of each segment from step 1 as shown to make a four-patch unit; press. Make 40.

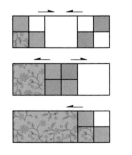

Make 40.

3. Sew together a light blue strip and a light green strip along the long edges to make a strip set; press. Make three strip sets. Subcut the strip sets into 40 segments, 2½" wide. Sew two segments together as shown to make a four-patch unit; press. Make 20.

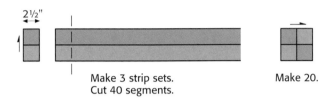

2½"

Make 3 strip sets.
Cut 40 segments.

Make 20.

4. Repeat step 3, using 2½"-wide white strips and light blue strips as shown. Make 20 four-patch units.

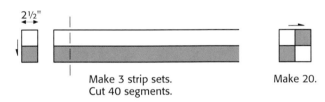

2½"

Make 3 strip sets.
Cut 40 segments.

Make 20.

5. Arrange and sew together two units from step 2, one unit each from steps 3 and 4, two 4½" white squares, one 4½" focus-print square, and one 4½" x 8½" focus-print rectangle as shown; press. Make 20 and label them block 4.

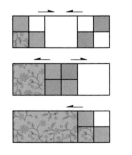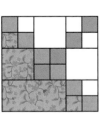

Block 4.
Make 20.

Assembling the Quilt

1. Arrange blocks 1–4 and the remaining 4½" x 8½" focus-print rectangles to make nine sections, taking care to orient the blocks as shown. Working with one section at a time, sew the blocks and rectangles together into horizontal rows; press. Sew the rows together; press. Make two each of sections 1, 2, and 4, and one each of sections 3, 3a, and 5.

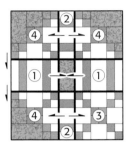

Section 1.
Make 2.

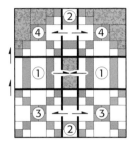

Section 2.
Make 2.

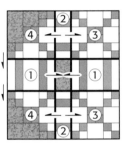

Section 3.
Make 1.

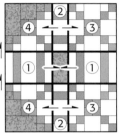

Section 3a.
Make 1.

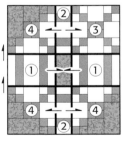

Section 4.
Make 2.

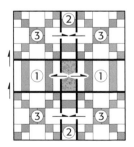

Section 5.
Make 1.

2. Arrange the sections from step 1 in three horizontal rows of three sections each as shown in the assembly diagram. Sew the sections together into rows; press. Sew the rows together; press.

3. Sew the accent strips end to end to make one continuous strip. From this long strip, cut two strips, 2½" x 96½", for the side inner borders, and two strips, 2½" x 88½", for the top and bottom inner borders. Sew the appropriate borders to the sides and then to the top and bottom of the quilt top. Press the seams toward the border.

4. Sew the 4½"-wide focus-print strips end to end to make one continuous strip. From this long strip, cut two strips, 4½" x 100½", for the side outer borders, and two strips, 4½" x 96½", for the top and bottom outer borders. Sew the appropriate borders to the sides and then to the top and bottom of the quilt top. Press the seams toward the border.

Finishing the Quilt

1. Layer the backing, batting, and quilt top; baste.

2. Hand or machine quilt as desired.

3. Refer to "Making Painless Mitered Binding" on page 12 and use the 2½"-wide focus-print strips to bind the quilt edges.

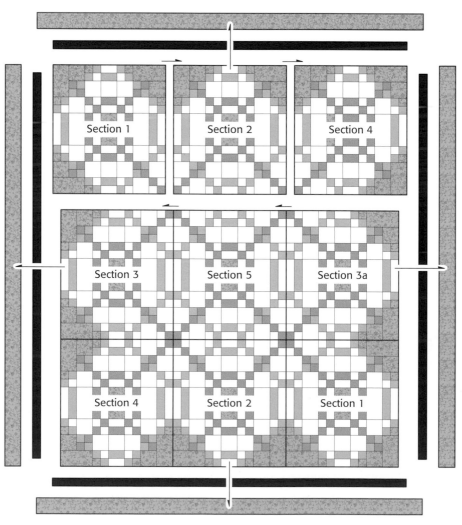

Assembly diagram

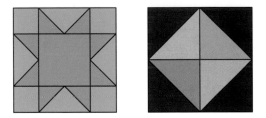

Finished quilt size: 56½" x 56½"
Finished block size: 8" x 8"

Materials

Yardage is based on 42"-wide fabric.

- 2⅛ yards *total* of assorted dark and light fabrics for Star blocks and outer border

- 1⅓ yards *total* of additional assorted light fabrics for alternate blocks and border blocks

- ⅓ yard of red fabric for alternate blocks and border blocks

- ⅓ yard of green fabric for alternate blocks and border blocks

- ½ yard of fabric for binding

- 3½ yards of fabric for backing

- 62" x 62" piece of batting

Cutting

All measurements include ¼"-wide seam allowances. Cut all strips across the width of the fabric.

Fabric	First Cut	Second Cut
Assorted darks and lights	13 squares, 4½" x 4½" (A)	
	6 strips, 4½" wide, for outer border	
	A *total* of 13 strips, 2½" wide	104 half-square triangles in matching sets of 8 (B)
		52 quarter-square triangles in matching sets of 4 (C)
		52 squares, 2½" x 2½", in matching sets of 4 (D)
Additional assorted lights	A *total* of 9 strips, 4½" wide	72 half-square triangles (E)
		20 squares, 4½" x 4½" (G)
Green	2 strips, 4½" wide	40 half-square triangles (F)
Red	2 strips, 4½" wide	32 half-square triangles (F)
Binding	6 strips, 2½" wide	

Making the Blocks

Refer to page 11 for tips on sewing an accurate ¼" seam allowance. You will make a total of 25 blocks for this quilt: 13 Star blocks and 12 alternate blocks. In addition, you will make 12 border blocks.

Star Blocks

Each block uses two contrasting fabrics: one for the background and one for the star motif. Occasionally swap placement of the light and dark fabrics within a block.

1. Sew matching B half-square triangles to each short side of a C quarter-square triangle as shown. Make four matching units.

Make 4.

2. Sew a unit from step 1 between two matching D squares as shown; press. Make two. Sew an A square between the remaining two units from step 1; press.

Make 2.

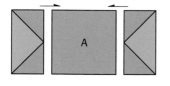
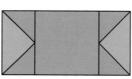

3. Arrange and sew the units from step 2 together as shown; press.

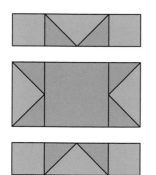
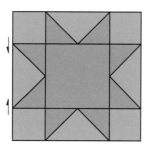

4. Repeat steps 1–3 to make a total of 13 blocks.

Alternate Blocks

Each block uses four scrappy additional light half-square triangles, two green half-square triangles, and two red half-square triangles.

1. Sew a light E half-square triangle and a green F half-square triangle together as shown; press. Make 40. Repeat, substituting the red F half-square triangles for the green triangles. Make 32.

Make 40.   Make 32.

2. Arrange two green/light units and two red/light units from step 1, carefully positioning the units as shown. Sew the units together to complete the block; press. Make 12. You'll use the rest of the units for the border blocks.

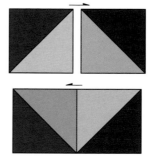
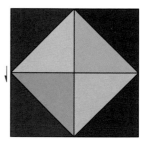

Make 12.

Border Blocks

Sew together two remaining red/light half-square-triangle units as shown; press. Make four. Repeat, using the remaining green/light half-square-triangle units. Make eight.

Make 4.

Make 8.

Assembling the Quilt

1. Arrange the Star and alternate blocks, the border blocks, and the G squares in horizontal rows, positioning the alternate and border blocks so they form large secondary stars as shown in the assembly diagram. Sew the blocks and squares together into rows; press. Sew the rows together; press.

2. Cut and sew 4½"-wide strips of random length from the remaining light and dark fabrics to make the borders. Make two borders, 4½" x 48½", piecing them with diagonal seams. Refer to the quilt photo on page 73 and sew the borders to the sides of the quilt. Press the seams toward the border. Make two borders, 4½" x 56½", and sew

them to the top and bottom; press. Note that the direction of the seams for the top and bottom borders is opposite those for the side borders. This enables all the seams to run in the same direction when the borders are sewn to the quilt.

Finishing the Quilt

1. Layer the backing, batting, and quilt top; baste.

2. Hand or machine quilt as desired.

3. Refer to "Making Painless Mitered Binding" on page 12 and use the 2½"-wide strips to bind the quilt edges.

Assembly diagram

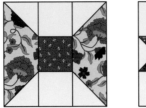
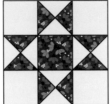

Finished quilt size: 84½" x 108½"
Finished block size: 12" x 12"

Materials

Yardage is based on 42"-wide fabric.

- 5 yards *total* of assorted light fabrics for blocks and pieced borders
- 3½ yards of focus print for blocks and outer border
- 2⅔ yards *total* of assorted dark fabrics for blocks and pieced borders
- ½ yard of accent fabric for blocks and pieced-border cornerstones
- 1 yard of fabric for binding
- 9½ yards of fabric for backing (vertical seams); 7½ yards (horizontal seams)
- 90" x 114" piece of batting

Cutting

All measurements include ¼"-wide seam allowances. Cut all strips across the width of the fabric.

Fabric	First Cut	Second Cut
Assorted lights	A *total* of 26 strips, 4½" wide	170 squares, 4½" x 4½" (24 in matching sets of 4; 102 in matching sets of 6) (A)
		10 rectangles, 4½" x 12½" (G)
	A *total* of 22 strips, 2½" wide	304 quarter-square triangles (144 in matching sets of 8) (B)
Assorted darks	A *total* of 7 strips, 4½" wide	54 squares, 4½" x 4½" (48 in matching sets of 4) (C)
	A *total* of 22 strips, 2½" wide	304 quarter-square triangles in matching sets of 10 (D)
Focus print	16 strips, 4½" wide	48 rectangles, 4½" x 12½" (E)
	10 strips, 4½" wide, for outer border	
Accent	3 strips, 4½" wide	21 squares, 4½" x 4½" (F)
Binding	11 strips, 2½" wide	

Making the Blocks

Refer to page 11 for tips on sewing an accurate ¼" seam allowance. You will make a total of 35 blocks: 18 Star blocks in two color variations and 17 Spool blocks.

Spool Blocks

1. Sew an F square between two matching A squares as shown; press. Make 17.

Make 17.

2. Referring to "Making Flippy Corners" on page 11 and with right sides together, align a matching A square on opposite ends of one E rectangle as shown. Sew, trim, and press. Make 48.

Make 48.

3. Sew a unit from step 1 between two units from step 2 as shown. Make 17. Set the remaining step 2 units aside for the pieced border.

Make 17.

Star Blocks

You need 18 Star blocks for this quilt: 12 of Star block 1 and 6 of Star block 2. Each block requires two fabrics: one light and one dark. In Star block 1, the dark fabric is the background. In Star block 2, the light fabric is the background.

1. Sew a B quarter-square triangle and a D quarter-square triangle together as shown; press. Make eight matching units.

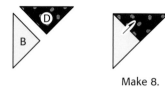

Make 8.

2. Sew two units from step 1 together as shown; press. Make four.

Make 4.

3. Sew a unit from step 2 between two matching C squares as shown; press. Make two. Sew a matching A square between the remaining two units from step 1; press.

Make 2.

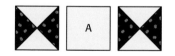 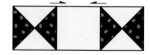

4. Arrange and sew the units from step 3 together as shown; press.

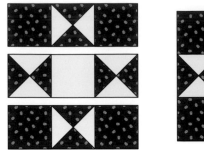

Star block 1

5. Repeat steps 1–4 to make a total of 12 blocks and label them Star block 1.

6. Repeat steps 1–4, substituting four matching A squares and 1 matching C square and turning the step 2 units as shown. Make six and label them Star block 2.

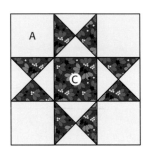

Star block 2.
Make 6.

Assembling the Quilt

1. Arrange the Star blocks and Spool blocks in seven horizontal rows of five blocks each, alternating and rotating them as shown in the assembly diagram on page 81. Sew the blocks together into rows; press. Sew the rows together; press.

2. Sew four remaining Spool units and three G rectangles together to make a pieced inner border; press. Make two and sew them to the sides of the quilt. Press the seams toward the border. Sew three remaining Spool units, two G rectangles, and two A squares together. Make two and sew them to the top and bottom; press.

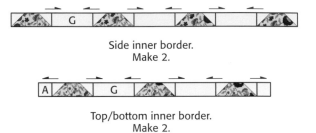

Side inner border.
Make 2.

Top/bottom inner border.
Make 2.

3. Sew two remaining B quarter-square triangles and two remaining D quarter-square triangles together as shown; press. Make 80.

Make 80.

4. Sew 23 units from step 3 together as shown; press. Make two and sew them to the sides of the quilt. Press the seams toward the newly added pieced border. Sew two F squares and 17 units from step 3 together as shown; press. Make two and sew them to the top and bottom; press.

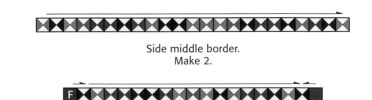

Side middle border.
Make 2.

Top/bottom middle border.
Make 2.

5. Sew the 4½"-wide focus-print strips together end to end to make one long strip. From this long strip, cut two strips, 4½" x 100½", for the side borders, and two strips, 4½" x 84½", for the top and bottom borders. Sew the appropriate borders to the sides, then to the top and bottom of the quilt. Press the seams toward the newly added border.

Finishing the Quilt

1. Layer the backing, batting, and quilt top; baste.

2. Hand or machine quilt as desired.

3. Refer to "Making Painless Mitered Binding" on page 12 and use the 2½"-wide strips to bind the quilt edges.

Assembly diagram

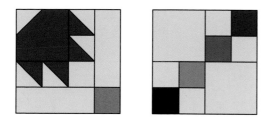

Finished table topper size: 44½" x 44½"
Finished runner size: 44½" x 28½" (each)
Finished block size: 8" x 8"

Materials

Yardage is based on 42"-wide fabric.

For either option:
- 1 yard of light fabric for blocks
- ⅝ yard *total* of assorted dark fabrics for blocks

Plus, for table topper:
- ¾ yard of focus print for outer border
- ½ yard of contrasting fabric for inner border
- ½ yard of fabric for binding
- 2⅞ yards of fabric for backing
- 50" x 50" piece of batting

Plus, for runners:
- 1 yard of focus print for outer border
- ½ yard of contrasting fabric for inner border
- ⅔ yard of fabric for binding
- 3 yards of fabric for backing
- 2 pieces, 34" x 50", of batting

This pattern calls for 16 blocks: eight Leaf blocks and eight Chain blocks. Option 1 uses all 16 blocks plus borders to make a table topper. Option 2 uses 16 blocks plus borders to make two runners. Fabric amounts and cutting for the blocks are the same for either option. Fabric amounts and cutting for inner and outer borders, binding, backing, and batting differ and are listed separately.

Cutting

All measurements include ¼"-wide seam allowances. Cut all strips across the width of the fabric.

Fabric	First Cut	Second Cut
Light	2 strips, 4½" wide	16 squares, 4½" x 4½" (G)
	8 strips, 2½" wide	32 half-square triangles (C)
		48 squares, 2½" x 2½" (B)
		16 rectangles, 2½" x 6½" (E)
Assorted dark prints	1 strip, 4½" wide	A *total* of 8 squares, 4½" x 4½" (A)
	A *total* of 5 strips, 2½" wide	32 half-square triangles in matching sets of 4 (D)
		40 squares, 2½" x 2½" (F)
Table Topper		
Contrasting fabric	4 strips, 2½" wide	
Focus print	5 strips, 4½" wide	
Binding	5 strips, 2½" wide	
Runners		
Contrasting fabric	6 strips, 2½" wide	
Focus print	7 strips, 4½" wide	
Binding	8 strips, 2½" wide	

Making the Blocks

Refer to page 11 for tips on sewing an accurate ¼"
seam allowance.

Leaf Blocks

1. Referring to "Making Flippy Corners" on page
   11 and with right sides together, align a B square
   on one corner of each A square as shown. Sew,
   trim, and press as shown. Make eight.

Make 8.

2. Sew a C half-square triangle and a D half-square
   triangle together as shown; press. Make 32 in
   matching sets of four.

Make 32
in matching
sets of 4.

3. Sew two matching units from step 2 together as
   shown; press. Make eight of each.

Make 8 of each.

4. Sew a unit from step 3 to the right edge of a
   matching unit from step 1 as shown; press. Make
   eight.

Make 8.

5. Sew a B square to the right edge of each remaining unit from step 3; press. Make eight. Sew a
   matching unit to the bottom edge of each unit
   from step 4; press.

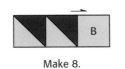

Make 8.

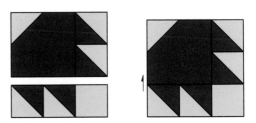

6. Sew an E rectangle to the right edge of each unit
   from step 5; press. Make eight.

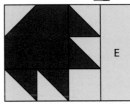

Make 8.

7. Sew an E rectangle to an F square as shown;
   press. Sew to the bottom edge of each unit from
   step 6; press. Make eight.

Make 8.

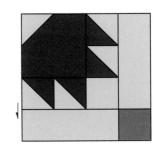
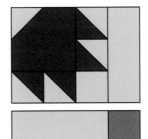

Make 8.

Chain Blocks

1. Arrange two B squares and two scrappy F squares as shown. Sew the squares together into rows; press. Sew the rows together; press. Make 16.

Make 16.

2. Arrange two units from step 1 and two G squares as shown. Sew the units and squares together into rows; press. Sew the rows together; press. Make eight.

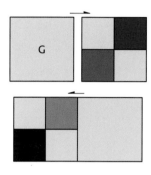

Make 8.

Assembling the Table Topper

1. Arrange the Leaf and Chain blocks in four horizontal rows of four blocks each as shown in the assembly diagram. Sew the blocks into rows; press. Sew the rows together; press.

2. Trim two 2½"-wide contrasting strips to measure 2½" x 32½" and sew them to the sides of the table topper; press. Trim the remaining 2½"-wide contrasting strips to measure 2½" x 36½" and sew them to the top and bottom; press.

3. Sew the 4½"-wide focus-print strips end to end to make one continuous strip. From this long strip, cut two strips, 4½" x 36½", for the side borders, and two strips, 4½" x 44½", for the top and bottom borders. Sew the appropriate borders to the sides and then to the top and bottom of the quilt top. Press the seams toward the border.

Assembly diagram

Assembling the Runners

1. Arrange the Leaf and Chain blocks in two horizontal rows of four blocks each as shown in one of the runner assembly diagrams on page 86. Sew the blocks into rows; press. Sew the rows together; press. Repeat for the second runner, using the alternate assembly diagram.

2. For each runner, trim one 2½"-wide contrasting strip into two 2½" x 16½" strips and sew them to the sides of the runner; press. Trim two 2½"-wide contrasting strips to measure 2½" x 36½" and sew them to the top and bottom; press.

3. Sew the 4½"-wide focus-print strips end to end to make one continuous strip. For each runner, cut two strips, 4½" x 20½", for the side borders, and two strips, 4½" x 44½", for the top and bottom borders. Sew the appropriate borders to the sides and then to the top and bottom of the runner. Press the seams toward the border.

Finishing the Table Topper or Runners

1. Layer the backing, batting, and topper or runner top; baste.

2. Hand or machine quilt as desired.

3. Refer to "Making Painless Mitered Binding" on page 12 and use the 2½"-wide strips to bind the edges.

Assembly diagrams

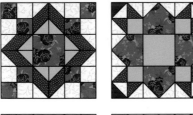

Finished quilt size: 64½" x 64½"
Finished block size: 24" x 24"

Materials

Yardage is based on 42"-wide fabric.

- 2⅞ yards of light fabric for blocks and borders
- 1⅞ yards of brown floral for blocks and borders
- 1 yard of dark green fabric for blocks and borders
- ⅔ yard of red fabric for blocks
- ¼ yard of light green fabric for blocks
- ⅝ yard of fabric for binding
- 3⅞ yards of fabric for backing
- 70" x 70" piece of batting

Cutting

All measurements include ¼"-wide seam allowances. Cut all strips across the width of the fabric.

Fabric	First Cut	Second Cut
Light	5 strips, 4½" wide	16 squares, 4½" x 4½" (A)
		16 rectangles, 4½" x 6½" (G)
	26 strips, 2½" wide	96 squares, 2½" x 2½" (B)
		36 rectangles, 2½" x 4½" (C)
		92 half-square triangles (D)
		56 quarter-square triangles (F)
		16 rectangles, 2½" x 6½" (H)
Brown floral	5 strips, 4½" wide	6 squares, 4½" x 4½" (A)
		56 half-square triangles (E)
	7 strips, 4½" wide, for outer border	
	2 strips, 2½" wide	8 squares, 2½" x 2½" (B)
		4 rectangles, 2½" x 4½" (C)
		4 quarter-square triangles (F)
Dark green	11 strips, 2½" wide	40 rectangles, 2½" x 4½" (C)
		24 half-square triangles (D)
		64 quarter-square triangles (F)
Red	8 strips, 2½" wide	4 squares, 2½" x 2½" (B)
		32 rectangles, 2½" x 4½" (C)
		44 half-square triangles (D)
		8 quarter-square triangles (F)
Light green	2 strips, 2½" wide	20 squares, 2½" x 2½" (B)
		1 square, 4½" x 4½" (A)
Binding	7 strips, 2½" wide	

Making the Blocks

Refer to page 11 for tips on sewing an accurate ¼"
seam allowance. Each block features a different
center design. You will sew together center blocks 1,
2, 3, and 4, then set them aside while you make the
outer sections of the large 24" blocks.

Center Block 1

1. Referring to "Making Flippy Corners" on page
   11 and with right sides together, align a light B
   square on one end of a dark green C rectangle,
   and a light green B square on the other end of
   the rectangle as shown. Sew, trim, and press.
   Make four of each.

Make 4 of each.

2. Sew one of each unit from step 1 together as
   shown; press. Make four.

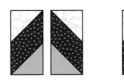

Make 4.

3. Arrange and sew two floral B squares and two
   light B squares together as shown; press. Make
   four four-patch units.

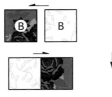

Make 4.

4. Arrange the units from steps 2 and 3 and one
   floral A square in three rows as shown. Sew the
   units and square into rows; press. Sew the rows
   together; press.

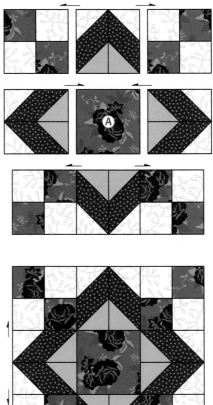

Center block 1

Center Block 2

1. Referring to "Making Flippy Corners" on page 11 and with right sides together, align a light B square with one corner of a floral A square as shown. Sew, trim, and press. Repeat to add a light B square to an adjacent corner of the unit; press. Make four.

Make 4.

2. Sew a light D half-square triangle and a dark green D half-square triangle together as shown; press. Make eight.

Make 8.

3. Repeat step 2, using light D half-square triangles and red D half-square triangles; press. Make four.

Make 4.

4. Arrange and sew two units from step 2, one unit from step 3, and a light green B square as shown; press. Make four.

Make 4.

5. Arrange the units from steps 1 and 4 and a light green A square in three rows as shown. Sew the units and square into rows; press. Sew the rows together; press.

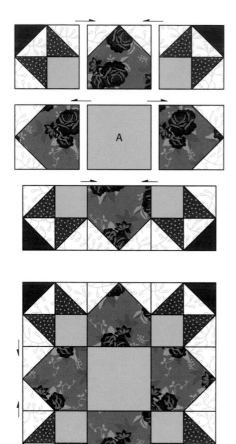

Center block 2

Center Block 3

1. Referring to "Making Flippy Corners" on page 11 and with right sides together, align a light B square with opposite corners of a floral A square as shown. Sew, trim, and press. Repeat to add a light B square to the remaining corners of the unit; press.

2. Referring to "Making Flippy Corners," sew a light green B square to one end of a light C rectangle as shown. Make four.

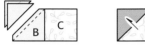

Make 4.

3. Sew a red B square to a light B square as shown; press. Make four. Sew each unit to a unit from step 2; press. Make four.

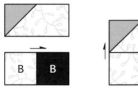

Make 4.

4. Sew a red D half-square triangle to each short side of a light F quarter-square triangle as shown; press. Make four.

Make 4.

5. Sew a floral C rectangle to a unit from step 4 as shown; press. Make four.

Make 4.

6. Arrange the units from steps 1, 3, and 5 in three rows, rotating the step 3 units as shown. Sew the units into rows; press. Sew the rows together; press.

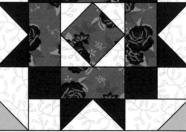

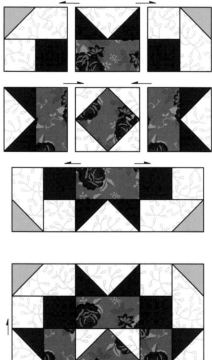

Center block 3

Center Block 4

1. Sew a light D half-square triangle and a red D half-square triangle together as shown; press. Make 16.

Make 16.

2. Sew a light F quarter-square triangle and a dark green F quarter-square triangle together as shown; press. Make four. Sew each unit to a floral E half-square triangle as shown; press. Make four.

Make 4.

3. Sew two units from step 1 together as shown; press. Make four of each.

Make 4 of each.

4. Sew a unit from step 3 to the top edge of a unit from step 2 as shown; press. Make four.

Make 4.

5. Sew a light green B square to each remaining unit from step 3; press. Make four. Sew one unit to the left edge of each unit from step 4; press. Make four.

Make 4.

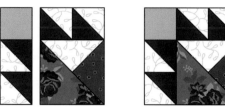

Make 4.

6. Arrange the units from step 5 into two rows of two units each as shown. Sew the units together into rows; press. Sew the rows together; press.

Center block 4

Making the Large Star Blocks

As you work through the next steps, you will be making the large outer star tips: two green and two red.

1. Sew a light D half-square triangle to each short side of a dark green F quarter-square triangle as shown; press. Make eight. Repeat, substituting red F triangles for the green F triangles. Make eight.

Make 8 of each.

2. Sew a light A square to each unit from step 1 as shown; press. Make eight with each color.

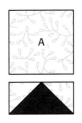

Make 8 of each.

3. Sew a light D half-square triangle and a dark green D half-square triangle together as shown; press. Make 16. Repeat, substituting red D triangles for the green D triangles. Make 16.

Make 16 of each.

4. Referring to "Making Flippy Corners" on page 11 and with right sides together, align a light B square on opposite ends of a dark green C rectangle as shown. Sew, trim, and press. Make eight of each. Repeat, substituting red C rectangles for the green C rectangles. Make eight of each.

Make 8 of each.

5. Sew a matching unit from step 3 to each unit from step 4, taking care to orient the units as shown. Make eight of each in each color combination.

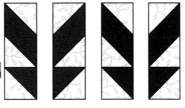

Make 8 of each.

6. Sew a light C rectangle and a dark green C rectangle together with a diagonal seam as shown; press. Make eight of each. Repeat, substituting red C rectangles for the green C rectangles. Make eight of each.

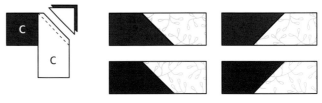

Make 8 of each.

7. Sew one light H rectangle to one light G rectangle as shown; press. Make 16.

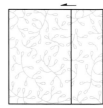

Make 16.

8. Working with one color (green or red) at a time, arrange and sew one of each unit from step 5, one of each unit from step 6, and a unit from step 2 as shown; press. Make eight of each color.

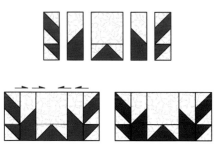

Make 8 of each.

9. Sew center block 1 between two red units from step 8; press. Repeat, using center block 2. Sew center block 3 between two green units from step 8; press. Repeat, using center block 4.

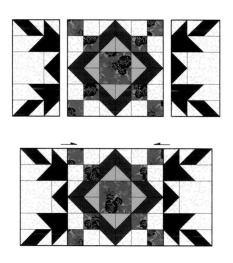

10. Again working with one color at a time, arrange four units from step 7, two units from step 8, and a unit from step 9 as shown. Sew the units into

rows; press. Sew the rows together. Make four blocks: two red and two green.

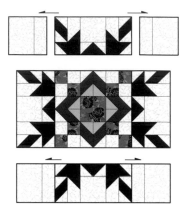

Assembling the Quilt

1. Arrange the red and green Star blocks in two rows of two blocks each, placing the colors as shown in the assembly diagram. Sew the blocks together into rows; press. Sew the rows together; press.

Assembly diagram

2. Sew a light F quarter-square triangle and a dark green F quarter-square triangle together as shown; press. Make 48. Sew each unit to one floral E half-square triangle as shown; press. Make 48.

Make 48.

3. Sew a floral F quarter-square triangle and a dark green F quarter-square triangle together as shown; press. Make four. Sew each unit to a floral E half-square triangle as shown; press. Make four.

Make 4.

4. Sew 12 units from step 2 together as shown; press. Make four pieced-border units. Sew a unit to the top and bottom of the quilt, carefully orienting the units as shown at right. Press the seams toward the pieced borders.

Make 4.

5. Sew a unit from step 3 to opposite ends of each remaining unit from step 4 as shown; press. Make two and sew them to the sides of the quilt; press.

Make 2.

6. Sew the 4½"-wide floral strips end to end to make one continuous strip. From this long strip, cut two strips, 4½" x 56½", for the side outer borders, and two strips, 4½" x 64½", for the top and bottom outer borders. Sew the appropriate borders to the sides and then to the top and bottom of the quilt top. Press the seams toward the newly added border.

Finishing the Quilt

1. Layer the backing, batting, and quilt top; baste.

2. Hand or machine quilt as desired.

3. Refer to "Making Painless Mitered Binding" on page 12 and use the 2½"-wide strips to bind the quilt edges.

About the Author

Although Cathy Wierzbicki has been a dedicated quilter since the mid-1990s, quilting is just one of her many interests. Her favorite pastime of all is spending time at a Minnesota lake with her husband, Tom, their two grown children, and one very special grandson.

Cathy currently makes her home in the Pacific Northwest. She has three other books to her credit, including *Coffee-Time Quilts: Super Projects, Sweet Recipes* (Martingale & Company, 2004), and she is the creator of the All-in-One Ruler™.